Loving Trump, Hating Trump
A Jewish Community Divided Against Itself

by Richard Borah

I0171302

Thou shall not hate thy brother in thine heart
Leviticus 19:17

Cruel is the strife of brothers.
Aristotle

Loving Trump, Hating Trump
A Jewish Community Divided Against Itself

Table of Contents

Introduction 4
Chapter 1: Donald the Destroyer 9
Chapter 2: American Nationalism 15
Chapter 3: Zio-nationalism Part 1 24
Chapter 4: Zio-nationalism Part 2 30
Chapter 5: Zio-nationalism Part 3 36
Chapter 6: The Jewish Anti-Trump Majority Pro-Trump Minority 43
Chapter 7: Schiff and Nadler: Dynamic Duo of Anti-Trumpism 50
Chapter 8: Democrats Spurn AIPAC While Republican Zionism Endures 56
Chapter 9: Will Democratic Progressivism Turn American Jewry to the Right? 65
Chapter 10: Who Gets to Define Morality in Trump's America? 73
Chapter 11: The Varieties of American Anti-Semitic Experiences 80
Chapter 12: Donald and Jared—An American Pharaoh and His Joseph 89
Chapter 13: Competing for the Victim Prize in Trump's America 96
Chapter 14: Understanding Trumpspeak—A Jewish Perspective 107
Chapter 15: When Donald Met Bernie: The New Socialist Chic and the American Jewish Community 118
Chapter 16: Democratic De-Zionation and Trump's Israeli Romance 129
Chapter 17: Trump's Love of Walls—Holy and Unholy 139
Chapter 18: Trump's Hyper-Masculinity Versus the Jewish Feminist Mystique 151

Chapter 19: Will a Trump Impeachment Be Blamed on the Jews? 165
Chapter 20: The Jewish Face of President Trump's Impeachment 176
Chapter 21: Trump, Governmental Lawlessness, and the Jewish (Not So) Civil War 185
Conclusion 204

Introduction

Loving Trump, Hating Trump
A Jewish Community Divided Against Itself

The Jewish community is experiencing an impassioned love-hate relationship with President Donald Trump and his policies. Question: Is POTUS 45 the American Jews' Guardian Angel or their Angel of Death? Has he been sent by the Almighty to save Israeli Jews from an Iranian nuclear nightmare and American Jews from the perils of hyper-leftism, or has he risen to punish the Jews by stoking the flames of anti-Semitism that often accompany fervent nationalist revivals? Is he a powerful leader who bluntly "tells it like it is" or the biggest liar who ever occupied the presidency? Well, it REALLY depends on who you ask.

The intensity and hardening of the pro-Trump and anti-Trump camps within the Jewish community has also created a level of intra-community anger and discord that is, in my opinion, unprecedented in recent times and highly destructive. The American Jewish community is currently at war with itself. There is a deep reservoir of fear and loathing by the Jewish Trumpers for the Jewish anti-Trumpers and vice versa. The result of this in-fighting is an American Jewish community that is substantially weakened and more vulnerable to its enemies, diminished in its ability to work effectively toward its own collective success, support the security of the State of Israel, and assist Jewish communities throughout the world.

This book will explore the sides of this ongoing battle with the hope of creating a bridge to understanding and a cooperative co-existence between the anti-Trumpers and their pro-Trump Jewish brethren. To that end, I will not be "siding" with any political point of view regarding President Trump and his policies. But by methodically and dispassionately presenting the rationale and perspective of each of the different perspectives, the hope is that the book will assist those on either side of the Trump debate with the ability to see the opposing one as having some rationale, and of being more than simply delusional, stupid, or evil.

At the heart of this deeply divided perspective is the 20th and 21st centuries' transformation of the Jewish people from a marginalized group of persecuted wanderers and sojourners into a people in possession of a powerful Jewish state and an unprecedented growth in its economic prowess and political influence in the U.S. and internationally. For the past 2000 years the Jews were a landless people whose status and rights were at the mercy of the dominant religious and ethnic groups in the countries where they sought refuge—often following frantic flights from varied state-sponsored exiles or slaughters. This historic persecution climaxed in the Holocaust and the annihilation of six million Jews.

Two thousand years of this unfathomably insecure existence have inculcated in the Jewish people a profound empathy for all oppressed peoples who have experienced, in some way, persecution and injustice, regardless of their religion or national background. In more recent times Jews have been at the forefront of civil rights and other liberal causes promoting the universal value and dignity of every human being.

It is the Jewish people's history, religion, and traditions that have provided them with a powerful desire to help those in need. This, in part, is why Jews in the U.S. are its most overwhelmingly liberal group. The 2013 Pew Research Center study of the U.S. Jewish community found that 49% of the American Jewish community self-identified as liberals, compared to 21% in the general population. But this enduring Jewish profile as the leading proponents of liberalism and universalism has been challenged as of late by four recent historical developments:

1. The establishment and growth of the State of Israel into a major international economic and military power.
2. The growing participation and influence of orthodox Jews and Israeli-American Jews in the U.S. economy and its government.
3. Changes that have taken place in the ideological positions of the American liberal leadership in the U.S. and abroad to more extreme positions (e.g., socialism, anti-Zionism) which many in the Jewish community view as being contrary to their interests and values.
4. The rise of militant Islamic terrorism as an enduring national and international threat.

These four factors have resulted in the growth of a nationalist sector of the U.S. Jewish population, many of which are aligned, to various degrees, with the nationalist agenda of President Trump and who are deeply at odds with their liberal Jewish brethren. In the analysis that follows we will explore these four issues and see how the recent rise in U.S. nationalistic fervor has resulted in an unprecedented level of conflict and animosity between the different Jewish political and religious factions. To be clear, there have always been significant divisions in the Jewish community. But recent developments have created fervent, entrenched camps among the Jewish people who view those in the *other* Jewish camp as the enemy, depending on where they stand on Donald Trump, Israel, and a number of other issues such as immigration, abortion, environmental legislation, women's and LGBT rights.

We are living in the age of "the Great Jewish Divide" where the previous goodwill that resulted from being part of the larger Jewish people is no longer enough for one Jew to consider another Jew one of his or her "brethren." In the following chapters we will see some evidence of the growing polarity and demonization taking place between the different Jewish political camps. Although there was significant disagreement within the Jewish community recently regarding President Obama, who many fervent Zionists viewed as being no friend to Israel, the situation with President Trump is, in my opinion, much more intense and deeply felt.

The Jewish community often follows a course somewhat parallel to the general community where it resides. In this regard, the virile antagonism and conflict that currently exists between the left and right of America and between the Democratic and the Republican parties in the U.S. is reflected in the unprecedented level of loathing among individuals in different political and ideological groups within the Jewish community.

What is important to understand is that this hatred is deeply connected to what each camp sees as the correct and moral *Jewish* perspective. The liberal Jews view Judaism's essential character as being one of universalism, kindness, and concern for the stranger. The Torah states many times, "You will not oppress the stranger for you were strangers in the land of Egypt." From the liberal perspective, these core Jewish ideals are under attack by the nationalism of the Trump presidency. Orthodox Jews, on the other hand, emphasize Jewish issues of traditional family life, religious freedom, and Zionism. They see Trump as an ally in battling the powerful enemies, on the left, of these Jewish values.

The objective of this text is to present both perspectives with some depth and clarity, leaving it to the reader to reflect on the merits of each. Perhaps this endeavor will be helpful in decreasing the level of antagonism between those on different sides of the ideological spectrum.

Chapter 1
Donald the Destroyer

American Hires
a Political Assassin

The election of Donald J. Trump to the office of President of the United States has radically transformed the experience of day to day life for the people of this country. It seems to many like they are experiencing "the end of the world, as we know it," to quote a popular song. Although our country has gone through powerful shifts in political dogma and policy throughout its history, the system of American governance was, at least publicly, considered a noble and functional one by its leaders, though subject to a variety of differing interpretations.

Even the "Reagan Revolution," which brought a return to more conservative policies during the '80s and disparaged what it saw as federal government overreach, was well within the traditional debate of whether the state or the federal government should dominate certain government policies. This "state versus federal" debate has been at the core of American political governance from the time of the nation's inception. The original Federalists favoring a stronger national government were led by Washington, Adams, and Hamilton, while the old Democratic-Republicans, led by Jefferson and Madison, favored a more decentralized, state-centered structure.

But with Donald Trump it is different.

President Donald Trump's disdainful and unrestrained offhand statements about the American political system and its leaders show that he holds the current American governmental structure *itself* to be highly dysfunctional at best, and useless at worst. He seems to believe that he has been charged by the voters to reshape our country in ways that may radically alter the underlying principles that define contemporary America. Trump implies by his statements that we may have to "throw the bums out and start from scratch" to repair a broken system in a broken land. Almost nothing about the American government, for Donald Trump, is particularly sacred. Some prime examples of how he has "boldly gone where no president has gone before" in attacking foundations of the American system of governance include:

1- Disparaging the CIA and FBI as being of limited use and questionable competence.
2- Insulting America's generals and other military leaders as "pathetic losers" in their inability to defeat ISIS quickly enough.
3- Praising Russian leader Vladimir Putin as being a superior leader to President Obama.
4- Communicating directly with 50 million people through his Twitter account while characterizing the mainstream media as being purposely biased, dishonest, and untrustworthy.
5- Assembling a cabinet of billionaires and multimillionaires, often with amazingly little or no governing experience.
6- Bringing in Steve Bannon early in his presidency as the top White House strategist in spite of Bannon's promoting of the alt-right, which contains within its orbit some highly anti-Semitic, white-supremacist elements.

One could go on and on.

Trump's supporters claim that his overturning of the status quo will result in a new day for America in which life for all will be fairer, freer, and more prosperous. I am not taking a stand on whether Trump's approach bodes well or ill for the country— only that it is truly unprecedented.

The power behind the belief, or at least hope, held by so many, that Donald Trump can "make America great again" comes from a deep discontentedness with the current U.S. government and economy. Although President Obama was popular, tens of millions of Americans struggled economically under his administration and most Americans saw the country as "moving in the wrong direction " (68% in McClatchy-Marist Poll, April, 2016). The older and younger representatives of many American demographics have had deep concerns about America's future prosperity and security. Terrorism, automation, international competition, and a variety of immigration-related issues have made otherwise level-headed people willing to "give Trump the ball" as the new "Disrupter in Chief." Everyone else who ran for president, including Hillary Clinton, was viewed as too much a part of the system or, at least, too respectful of the system to "blow it to smithereens." Trump, whatever else you might say about him, does not seem to lack the capacity for creating mayhem and upheaval, which many believe to be necessary in order to make changes in a country that they view as having gone astray.

Nothing within the spheres of politics, economics, or personal relationships seems to be sacred for Donald Trump. Everything and everyone are potential targets. This is reflected in his manner of expressing himself in a variety of situations. Refusing to disavow his previous characterization of Rosie O'Donnell as "a fat pig" during the first national presidential debate comes to mind as a watershed moment in the breakdown of political civility in America, but there are so many other similar gems. Many of his statements are so unprecedented by a president when judged by the standards of professional political discourse (or even by the standards of basic adult norms) that, in spite of their unseemliness, they successfully signal that Donald Trump has no fear of dismantling even the deepest level of the American political system, with an utter contempt for "politics as usual." This lack of boundaries is one of the keys to Trump's unique appeal, and although many are shocked and appalled by the outrageous statements and Tweets, few fail to recognize that Trump is a force that cannot be controlled easily, if at all.

Donald Trump—Political Assassin

The election of Donald Trump resembled hiring a professional killer to carry out a contract on the American political system. When you hire a killer, you want one that has no scruples or boundaries of behavior that might impede carrying out the desired assassination. Donald Trump has been hired by a significant number of enraged, frightened, and betrayed white working-class and middle-class Americans to "kill" the American government status quo. And who better to murder it than a profoundly aggressive, cantankerous, outrageous, overbearing alpha-male who doesn't hold anything about American governance dear, and whose favorite pastime is beating his opponents into submission?

Maybe President Trump, if reelected, will be successful in fully restoring America's economic dominance and self-respect. The COVID-19 pandemic has thrown this possibility into great doubt. But even if he doesn't accomplish this, his fans believe that at least he will make the self-righteous and self-serving political leaders and their cronies all pay by taking apart their world and pulling off their masks of false morality and decency. These are the high-flying politicians, lobbyists, media personalities, and special interests who have made millions or billions off the American governmental system by capitalizing on access and special interests. Trump supporters have believed that he can disempower and shame them, so they can experience at least a small taste of the bitter defeat that has permeated the lives of "Trump's Americans" for decades.

The Jewish Community, Trump, and the Status Quo
How does the American and Israeli Jewish community view the U.S. government and Trump's upending of the status quo? This is a bit complicated. Regarding foreign policy, certainly Donald Trump has departed from the Obama administration's more trusting and conciliatory positions regarding Palestinian demands on Israel and with regards to the legitimacy of the Iranian government. Trump has boldly challenged Iran's nuclear ambitions and its genocidal stance toward the Jewish state. The Trump administration also has shown zero tolerance for what it views as Israel-bashing at the UN and is thought of by many Israelis and American Zionists as "the best friend Israel has ever had in the White House." So those in the Jewish community who are ardent Zionists, for the most part, approve of these profound foreign policy changes. Those Jewish community members, on the other hand, who are unsupportive of Israel's non-conciliatory stance toward the Palestinians regarding land or of Israeli security policies that restrict free movement of Palestinians and their commerce are also profoundly disdainful of the Trump administration's shift in policy. We will explore this area of transformation in the next two chapters.

What about domestic issues that the Trump presidency has powerfully impacted in its first three years? How does the American Jewish community view the Trump administration's recent rolling back of environmental legislation and agreements; its placing conservative judges onto the supreme courts and other courts; its seeking stronger measures to restrict illegal immigration; its calling into question the integrity of major press organizations? We now need to also consider the Jewish community's views on how Trump has handled the COVID-19 pandemic and its impact on America's health outcomes and its economic fallout.

In general, the highly liberal elements of the community balk at these changes. However, nothing succeeds like success, and if the U.S. economy returns to its pre-coronavirus boom with rising stock market prices, company earnings growth, increased wages, and low unemployment, I believe some of the liberal Jewish community's distaste for Trump's policies will be tempered by the improvements experienced in their pockets and pocketbooks. The Jews are a practical people and, regardless of their politics, a dramatically improved economy and its benefits to the lives of all will not be lost on them. But if the COVID-19 pandemic maintains its hold on the American and world economy come election day, people will have short memories of the recent "post-Trump bump." If come November 2020, President Donald Trump has succeeded in "making America rich again (again)" (great or not), a significant percentage of liberal Jews (and other liberals) will probably hold their nose and vote for him. We will have to wait and see how this drama plays out.

Chapter 2
American Nationalism
It Comes in Three Flavors

During the many centuries of Jewish community life among the nations of Europe, there is a clear pattern that has emerged: When nationalism has intensified in a country, anti-Semitism and Jewish persecution has increased. Nationalism replaced Christianity in the 19th and 20th centuries as the primary motivator of anti-Semitism. Nationalism is defined by the Merriam-Webster dictionary as:

> Loyalty and devotion to a nation; *especially*: a sense of national consciousness exalting one nation above all others and placing primary emphasis on promotion of its culture and interests as opposed to those of other nations or supranational groups.

But the Merriam-Webster's dictionary definition doesn't include the stimulation of anti-Semitism and the persecution of other minorities—a consistent correlate of nationalism.

This occurred in the 19th and first half of the 20th century in many European countries where the rise in nationalism resulted in the Jews and other minorities in these countries being viewed by nationalists as enemies or potential enemies of the state, or simply as inferior human beings. Jews and other minorities were subject to various levels of persecution, attack, and in the most extreme form, extermination. The Jew being distinct in religion, language, customs, and history was simply not considered to be a true patriot or loyal citizen. Add to this profile, the Jews' international cohesiveness as a people, and the profound distrust of Jews left over from hundreds of years of European Christian anti-Semitism, and the rise of European nationalism inevitably, resulted in Jews being intensely targeted as the most reviled non-national of all the minorities.

The question is whether the current rise of nationalism in the United States will take a form similar to that of Europe or, due to certain significant differences between America and Europe, as well as differences in the societal position of American Jews at the current time, will result in a different outcome from that of 19th and 20th century Europe. So, before American Jews run for cover or move to Israel or Canada, let's try to address the following three questions:

1- Does America's unique history and population make American nationalism different from the nationalism that plagued the Jewish people in Europe during the 19th and 20th centuries?

2- Will American Jews' strong economic and political position in the United States prevent American nationalism from resulting in persecutions similar to those that took place in Europe?

3- Does the fact that Jewish people have a nation of their own now, in Israel, affect the impact of American nationalism on the American Jewish community?

Let's start with the question of whether American nationalism is distinct because America is different from any other country in the world. What are the unique qualities of the United States that might mitigate against the more destructive dimensions of nationalism and, particularly, deter a rise in anti-Semitism?

The "national DNA" of America is fundamentally different from that of Europe. The United States does not have a history of the church or of Christianity ever being its governing power. The U.S. has never had a "middle ages" experience in which Jews were viewed as the pariah race and the murderers of the messiah and who Christians believe were experiencing the punishment they deserved due to this perceived ultimate evil. America was established upon the bedrock of religious freedom and the separation of church and state. I understand that America was founded as a Christian country, although not officially, and that Jews and other religious and racial minorities have experienced some degree of persecution here over the years. Also, racism is quite close to the core of the American psyche with black slavery being an issue that divided the country and eventually brought it to civil war and which led to segregation and other discriminatory laws and practices. However, in spite of these elements, America does not have the same "collective memory" as Europe of being a country whose very identity and roots were based in the Church and who for hundreds of years treated Jews with complete contempt.

These distinctions have mitigated against religious persecution and anti-Semitism in America and will most likely continue to do so. One caveat is the current fear and hatred of Muslims that has grown with the rise of 9/11 and Islamic terrorism. Whether this phenomenon will create a more general anti-outsider and anti-Semitic momentum is yet to be determined. However, the fact that the Jewish community is among the most strident supporters of liberal policies, which include support for border and immigration reform (75-80% of the Jewish population voted for Clinton and Obama), may put the Jews at a heightened risk of being seen as "aiding and abetting the enemy."

In October 2018, 11 Jewish attendees at the Tree of Life synagogue were murdered by Robert Bowers. Shortly before his shooting, Bowers posted a message on an alt-right social media site about his anger toward the refugee support group HIAS, formerly known as the Hebrew Immigrant Aid Society. HIAS is one of the nine national agencies that helps to resettle refugees in the United States and serves refugees of all faiths and nationalities. The shooter believed the Jewish nonprofit was helping transport members of the Central American migrant caravan into the United States, repeatedly referring to the caravan as "invaders" who want to "kill us."

America also lacks the deep "blood roots" of its European counterparts. It is true that there are families that have been in America from its beginning, but this group is very small and 250 years is not the same as 1,000 or 1,500 years of blood lineage found in Europe. Also, America was built by immigrants from so many different types who have created an amalgam of cultures and backgrounds that form the characteristic "melting pot" of American culture. Therefore, I believe that America is protected against the severity of racial nationalism that characterized a major dimension of the racism and anti-Semitic fervor of the nationalist movements in Europe during the 19th and early 20th century in countries such as Germany, France, and Italy. I am not suggesting that there won't be an increase in this type of anti-Semitism with the growth of nationalism. Only that it will be mitigated and lessened by America's unique history, ideals, and population makeup.

Unfortunately, there is a third powerful source of anti-Semitism that is also stimulated by the growth of nationalism. America, I believe, is as susceptible to this one as any European country. This is economic nationalism. Some might believe that economic issues were always the true motivators of religious and blood nationalism as well, with religion and race being convenient "beards" that masked feelings of economic jealousy, frustration, and fear. What is economic nationalism? Simply, the idea that a nation should put its own citizens' economic situation first and that any group that threatens or diminishes the economic success of the country must be stopped and dealt with harshly. An extreme example of this is found in the Biblical story of Sodom, in which Abraham's nephew Lot lived. In Sodom the most unforgivable crime was to assist a non-Sodomite citizen in any way, as it was viewed as diminishing the economic position of Sodom. To provide a meal for a poor non-Sodomite was a capital crime. It was Sodomites for Sodomites only!

I am certainly not equating the current rise of American nationalism with the cruelty of Sodom. However, the story of Sodom does bring out just how aggressive economic nationalism can be and how anybody who aides or assists "outsiders" to the detriment of the home country can be perceived as a dangerous enemy that must be stopped. It is here that the American Jewish community and each American Jew is vulnerable to a rise in anti-Semitism that accompanies the rise of economic nationalism.

The impact of the current COVID-19 pandemic on nationalist fervor needs to also be considered. There are two characteristics of this pandemic that will most likely energize and intensify the current rise in American nationalist feelings.

1-The identifying of the source of the coronavirus as China. There are discussions about whether it was a natural or a manufactured virus strain, some even speculating about a planned viral attack. Viewing of the pandemic as being the result of a Chinese virus that resulted in the death and sickness of thousands of Americans will weaponize nationalist feelings against China, our major economic rival, as well as toward other countries.

2-The major economic downturn of America that has resulted from the virus will likely intensify nationalist fervor. The U.S. economy as of this writing has gone from boom to bust and unemployment has shifted from the lowest level in history to one of the highest. The impact of this dramatic shift is yet to be determined but, historically, economic downturns foment nationalist feelings and, in its most toxic form, result in persecution and violence against those viewed as "outsiders." Without the post-World War II economic depression in Germany it is highly unlikely that Hitler and his racist, ultra-nationalist policies could have taken control of the country.

The nationalist fervor of President Trump and his most ardent followers is based on a belief that there are foreign and international forces that have been hollowing out the economy of the United States. For the most part these forces are large corporations and financial institutions that have adapted to a global economy and taken advantage of cheap labor, automation, and international markets, sometimes at the expense of local jobs and wages. This international approach is pursued by corporations and financial institutions to increase profits and not due to any disloyalty to America.

I don't think Trump or his supporters viewed Carrier Air Conditioner or Ford Motor Company as having anti-American intentions when they moved plants and jobs to Mexico. Trump and his supporters know the decision was based on economics and increasing the profits of the company. But this choosing of profits over keeping America affluent and strong is becoming the new definition of disloyalty and traitorous anti-American behavior. Once this line is crossed, and internationalizing of business operation is viewed as a lack of patriotism, then all those who are empowered in financial and business institutions may be viewed as unpatriotic. Their business interests and decisions, which will inevitably include moving of jobs and funds to other countries, may have a significantly heightened risk for anti-Semitic feelings against the Jewish community.

The Jews have grown economically and have become leaders in U.S. business and finance over the past 50 years. This results in many Jews having prominent corporate leadership positions at businesses and institutions that are highly international in their operations. Couple this with the underlying distrust of Jews as being an "international people" tied to other Jewish people throughout the world (echoes of the "Protocols of the Elders of Zion") and to the "start-up nation" of the State of Israel, and you have a potent mix for the stimulation of economic-based anti-Semitism. We will not be accused of being killers of the messiah. Nor will we, I believe, be accused of not having true American blood in our veins. The anti-Semitism will potentially grow from the perspective that the Jew is a central player in the internationalization of business, commerce and media and as being a group whose interest is more focused on the wealth and welfare of other Jews than that of America and Americans.

Due to this type of thinking, I am of the opinion that American Jews are in a time of growing risk of anti-Semitism in the U.S. A recently published report from the Anti-Defamation League

(ADL) bears this out.

> The American Jewish community experienced the highest level of antisemitic incidents last year since tracking began in 1979, with more than 2,100 acts of assault, vandalism and harassment reported across the United States, according to new data from ADL (the Anti-Defamation League). The record number of incidents came as the Jewish community grappled with vicious and lethal antisemitic attacks against communities in Poway, Jersey City and Monsey, and a spree of violent assaults in Brooklyn.

> The 2019 ADL Audit of Antisemitic Incidents, issued today, found that the total number of antisemitic incidents in 2019 increased 12 percent over the previous year, with a disturbing 56 percent increase in assaults. The audit found there were, on average, as many as six antisemitic incidents in the U.S. for each day in the calendar year— the highest level of antisemitic activity ever recorded by ADL. https://www.adl.org/news/press-releases/antisemitic-incidents-hit-all-time-high-in-2019

I think we have addressed our three original questions:

1- Contemporary America differs from Europe in a manner that mitigates against the risk of religious and blood racism.

2- America is not different from Europe regarding economic nationalism. Here it is on an equal plane with all other countries.

3- The American Jewish community's success in the United States does not protect us completely from the potential attack of economic racism. To the contrary, it makes us a bigger target as our success is well-known and widespread and seen as due to international connections.

As a closing thought, I would like to mention that some assume that since we are not the powerless, ostracized community we were in Europe, we can overcome any anti-Semitic threat through our own power and influence. This may be accurate and it is certainly something to consider. But though the Jewish community may have wealth and position, our numbers are still very small (approximately 2% of the U.S. population). It is certainly the case that the aggressiveness of anti-Semites and other bullies is stimulated by a weak victim, and it is possible that the current standing of the Jewish community as a force to be reckoned with will deter the attack of the economic anti-Semite. We can certainly hope that things play out this way.

Chapter 3
Zio-Nationalism Part 1
The Rise of the American-Jewish Nationalist

Donald Trump's presidency has created a new and exceptionally deep chasm in the already highly fractured American Jewish community. Put simply, the liberal American Jews loved Obama and loath Trump. The orthodox Jews and the Israeli-Americans mostly loathed Obama for his left-leaning positions and his clashes with Netanyahu, as well as for what they perceived as Obama's pro-Palestinian bias in his assessment of the Israeli-Palestinian conflict. However, many of these Zionist American Jews who were anti-Obama became enamored with candidate Trump and voted for him, in part due to his rejection of the political correctness of the left, his disdain for the UN's anti-Israel policies, and for his vocal, fervent support of Israel and its security concerns. As the *New York Times* reported on December 26, 2016, in the aftermath of an unprecedented failure of the U.S. to veto a UN resolution condemning Israeli settlements:

Mr. Obama's decision on Friday not to block a United Nations Security Council condemning Israeli settlements laid bare all the grievances the two men have nursed since shortly after they took office in 2009. For Mr. Netanyahu, it was the final betrayal by a president who was supposed to be an ally but never really was. For Mr. Obama, it was the inevitable result of Mr. Netanyahu's own stubborn defiance of international concerns with his policies. The two sides did little to hide their mutual contempt. After talks led them to conclude that Mr. Obama would not veto the resolution, as presidents of both parties have done in the past, Israeli officials essentially washed their hands of the incumbent and contacted his successor in the wings. President-elect Donald J. Trump promptly put out a statement calling on Mr. Obama to veto the resolution.

Regarding Trump there is no monolithic American Jewish perspective. However, with 71% of Jews voting for Clinton and only 24% of them voting for Trump, according to a *New York Times* exit poll, it is safe to say that the liberal American Jewish left still defines the Jewish community's political profile. Similarly, Breitbart.com reported that a higher percentage of Jews voted for Clinton than any other religious group. However, there are strong indications of orthodox Jews favoring Trump in the election. On November 10, 2016, the *New York Times* reported, "In Brooklyn's 48th Assembly District, which encompasses most of Borough Park, Mr. Trump got 69 percent of the vote, while Mrs. Clinton got 27 percent." https://www.nytimes.com/2016/11/11/nyregion/in-democratic-stronghold-of-new-york-city-trump-finds-support-among-orthodox-jews.html?_r=0

But the orthodox and Israeli-American community is a small percentage of the overall American Jewish community (perhaps 10-15%) and, beyond the New York metro area, lacks the size, influence, and power to define the American Jewish community's political profile. As we are discussing the potential impact of rising American nationalism on anti-Semitism, among other things, it is useful to reflect on the Trump supporters' impression of the

Jewish community as a whole. From their perspective the Jewish community is perceived, in spite of its complexities, as overwhelmingly and intensely Democratic in party affiliation, and liberal in political perspective. This obvious fact is sometimes lost to orthodox and Israeli-American Jews who interact with like-minded "Zionationalists" in their personal circles and their somewhat politically monolithic communities. In this sense the Jews, I believe, are generally viewed by MAGA supporters as the vanguard of anti-Trump liberalism and as leading the fight against his presidency's policies. Though some orthodox Jews and Israelis may strongly support Trump, this does not impact the overall impression the general population has of American Jews as "never Trumpers" and enemies of the "MAGA" agenda. American Jews are viewed as dead set against Clinton's "deplorables" who fervently support Trump's nationalism.

What about Zionism? The American Jewish support for the State of Israel is a factor that, on the one hand, makes the American Jews susceptible to nationalist-fueled anti-Semitism, since the Jew could be perceived as being more loyal to a foreign country (Israel) than the United States. On the other hand, Trump's almost unqualified support of Israel and the fervent Zionism of his evangelical Christian base has, to date, been a strong, consistent part of Trump's vision for American foreign policy. We need to drill down a bit here to tease out the tangled threads of meaning of this complex convergence of American Jewish Zionism, Trump's support of Israel, and the Trump-supporting American nationalist's view of how Zionism fits in.

To start, I would pose the simple idea that American nationalists identify and sympathize with other countries' nationalistic agendas. So, the "America first" Trumpbackers are supportive of the idea that an embattled country, like Israel, must look out for its own defense and economic interests first and put this before other more universalist issues (international human rights issues, diplomatic initiatives, etc.). From this point of view, the American nationalists and fervent Trump supporters strongly agree that Israel must primarily concern itself with its security before parsing out whether the settlements and the security measures taken against Palestinians adhere to universal norms of mercy and justice for all, and international standards of conduct. It is the nationalist rejection of the legitimacy of international standards of conduct touted by the UN, the E.U., and other world bodies that align Trump's nationalists with the Likud government's rejection of these bodies and their policies. American nationalists understand that Israel, like the United States, has to put itself first and that this consideration outweighs obedience to the pronouncements of any international bodies and their decisions about the nation's conduct and policies. Also, as a bonus for Israel, the Palestinians are grouped together by American nationalists, along with other Arab extremists and terrorist groups like ISIS, that are seen as a grave threat to the United States. As the saying goes, "the enemy of my enemy is my friend." So, American nationalists and the Israeli nationalists see eye to eye on both the policy of putting the country first over international edicts *and* in perceiving the Palestinians as part of a larger common enemy (militant Islam) to both their countries. Many American nationalists see the support of Israel as being in America's best interests, by being a reliable, militarily strong and staunch democracy in the Middle East. A February 12, 2019 article in the *Washington Free Beacon* states:

> The United States and Israel share security and economic interests, not just values, and pro-Israel voices need to highlight this point because they too often ignore it. First, the big picture: the Middle East is still very important to American national security, and Israel is the only Middle Eastern country where both the government and the people are pro-American.
> Whatever happens in the region, Israel will always be there, with its robust economy and military might, ready to help the United States. Moreover, Israel is on the front lines—literally—fighting America's enemies—Iran, Sunni jihadist groups, and others.

Does a nuclear-armed Iraq or Syria sound like a frightening prospect? Fortunately, it is still just a prospect rather than reality, because of Israeli military actions in 1981 and 2007. Unlike other U.S. allies, Israel has never asked for a single American soldier to deploy to Israel and give their life for the Jewish state. Israel has always been committed to defending itself. That is an invaluable strategic asset. More specifically, the United States benefits from its alliance with Israel in very practical ways. In 2012, Michael Eisenstadt and David Pollock, both fellows at the Washington Institute for Near East Policy, produced a great report that details these benefits — from intelligence sharing and counterterrorism cooperation to cyber and water security. Israel's remarkable technological innovation is critical for American businesses, and its expertise in homeland security and military tactics are critical for keeping Americans—both in and out of uniform—safe. https://freebeacon.com/blog/american-support-israel-based-strategic-interests-not-just-morality/

This military/security dimension is an important point of convergence between the American nationalists, led by Trump and the Israelis. The Jewish state is viewed by American nationalists as a strong military and economic partner that can be totally relied upon. Israel is an ally that makes America stronger and is a bulwark against the Islamic threat. So, from a purely American nationalistic perspective, a strong alliance with Israel is a big plus. This has nothing to do with a nationalist identification or appreciation of Israel. It's just that all the other allies or potential allies in the region are weak, unreliable, or both.

There is a difference between American nationalists' support of Israel and American nationalists' support of American Jews. They are far from the same thing. First of all, although many American Jewish liberals are pro-Israel, this does not at all mitigate against the mistrust that an American nationalist may have toward the

American Jewish liberal community. There are much larger issues that, for the American nationalist, puts the American Jewish liberal in the category of distrusted adversary. The fact that there may be some convergence on support of Israel between American nationalists and Jewish liberals does not impact or bridge this profound political, ideological divide, for either side. The American Jewish liberal is the adversary of the American nationalist for the following reasons:

1-The American Jewish liberals are viewed as internationalists whose political approach as well as business and economic interests do not converge with the "America first" agenda of the MAGA crowd.

2-American liberal Jews loathe Trump politically and personally.

3-The American liberal Jews were the strongest supporters of Obama/Clinton and their views and political positions.

4-The American liberal Jews are perceived as being at the heart of the liberal press, which is viewed as "fake," conspiratorial, and dedicated to destroying Trump and his MAGA agenda.

5-American liberal Jews are at the forefront of support for immigrants (illegal and legal) and their children. Cities with significant liberal Jewish communities often fall into the "Sanctuary Cities" group.

American nationalists and American Jewish liberals co-waving an Israeli flag will not make up any ground on these major, divisive issues. In a nutshell, the American Jewish liberal is the enemy of the American nationalists and every true-red Trump lover. But what about the orthodox and the American Israelis? How do they fare in MAGA country and with the alt-right?

It is true that the majority of orthodox American Jews and Israeli-Americans have favored and supported Trump. It is also true that orthodox Jews and Israeli-Americans have little love or patience for their American Jewish liberal community brethren and their "Obama/Clinton" political agenda. But does the alt-right or even the run-of-the-mill Trump fan really embrace these Trump-lovin' Jews? Not so fast! I think we need to go a bit deeper to analyze whether we have any common ground here or not.

Chapter 4
Zio-Nationalism Part 2

White Supremacists, the Alt-Right,
and the American-Jewish Nationalist

Richard Spencer achieved some notoriety as the rising star of white racism in the United States during the Trump campaign. The originator of the term "alt-right," Spencer is a transitional figure of this growing supremacist movement. A December 3, 2016 article by Tali Krupkin in the Israeli newspaper *Haaretz* describes the now well-known November 19, 2016 event that lifted Richard Spencer from obscurity to fame:

> The night Richard Spencer shouted "Hail Trump!" before a crowd of white men—who saluted with raised arms at a far-right conference in Washington—was the moment the 38-year-old leader of the so-called alt-right, a white nationalist movement, became known around the world.

The outraged reaction by the media to this Nazi salute to the new president was met with outrage and disgust from many fronts. But Spencer and the alt-right crowd claim to reject Nazism's anti-Semitism, though many people see this as being a strategy to achieving broader, mainstream appeal.

> "I want people to understand that we are not neo-Nazis," he (Spencer) repeats to Haaretz, saying he would not collaborate with any neo-Nazis at his events, adding, "I don't know any neo-Nazis that want to work with me, to be honest."

In spite of this somewhat tepid distancing of himself and the alt-right from Nazism, in an *Haaretz* interview Spencer unapologetically responded to push back from the "Hail Trump" incident:

> "I understand why people were offended, but they have to understand the context in which it happened. The context of fun and exuberance…. I actually don't regret it and I definitely don't condemn it," he continues. "This has made a wave in the media and there are many people who will start looking into the ideas of the alt-right, so it is ultimately a good thing."

Spencer also commented on Steve Bannon, who previously ran the Breitbart website, which is the most prominent forum for alt-right ideas, and who was formerly President Trump's chief strategist and senior counsel to the administration:

> "What I think happened is that Breitbart has been open to the alt-right ideas, it has been a platform for the alt-right. That is a very positive step. But I don't think Steve Bannon is an alt-right thinker."

Spencer does see the possibility of a white-nationalist America finding common ground with the State of Israel, which he views in a completely different light from the American Jewish liberal left. Spencer explains:

> "Your average eastern seaboard liberal Jew, who takes his marching orders from The New York Times and reads Phillip [sic] Roth in his spare time, will likely never want to have anything

to do with the far right—even if his life depended on it. Bibi
Netanyahu and Avigdor Lieberman are a different story…. Who
knows? Israeli nationalists might want to help finance the far right
in Europe and North America."

Strange Partners in the Hatred of Jewish Liberalism

Personally, I will err on the side of caution and not make much, if
any distinction, between Richard Spencer and the good ol' anti-
Semitic white supremacist, Nazi-sympathizing miscreants who
have plagued Jews and other groups forever. Right-leaning
American Jewish Zionists and their Israeli counterparts are at risk
of developing "Short Memory Disorder" regarding the well-
established historical association of nationalism and antisemitism.
No clear-headed Jewish Zionist should surmise that just because
the alt-right might agree with them in the rejection of certain of
the left's priorities and support a nationalistic Israel policy, that
that Zionist Jews can be "best buds" with Spencer and comrades.
Even if Spencer is not hiding anti-Semitic hatred and is sincere in
saying he has nothing against the Jews, (which I highly doubt), in
the end the Jews will utilize their power and influence to stand in
the way of the alt-right and obstruct their plans and actions. With
this, the Jews will quickly become an identified enemy of the alt-
right. And if there is one thing that Jewish faith and Jewish history
has taught, it is that the Jews are viewed by their enemies as a
single entity. Our connectedness to one another, sour
separateness as a people, and our uniqueness in religion, culture,
history, and perspective make this inevitable. Exceptions will not
be made for Jews who wear "I love Trump" or "I ALSO Hate
Liberals" buttons.

It is a mistake for the Jewish right, whether it be orthodox Jews,
Israeli-Americans, or just unaffiliated conservative, Republican-
leaning Jews, to demonize the Jewish liberal left. This will only
increase the fervor and success of people like Spencer who will
use this internal Jewish struggle to advance a cause that, if

successful, will bring back the former comfort zone for openly persecuting Jews, first in subtle forms, but slowly (or quickly) growing to more open and strident anti-Semitic acts. Liberal Jews as well must understand that in demonizing Israeli settlement policies that they view as unjust or aggressive, they are also aiding and abetting those who will not make a distinction between Bernie Sanders and Benjamin Netanyahu. As I stated, it is our fate, our destiny, and our challenge to always ultimately be viewed as a single people, a single force in the world.

The current movement of the liberal left to embrace such extreme positions, coupled with the election of Donald Trump, is creating a new level of distance and dissension between American Jews on the left with those on the right. It is this unprecedented disdain, one for the other, that has created the macabre spectacle of many liberal Jews seeing Israel and Israeli supporters as evil persecutors of what they perceive as the abused Palestinians. Meanwhile, the right-leaning fervent Israel and Trump-supporting Jews (mostly orthodox and Israeli-Americans) view these left-leaning Jews as somewhere between insane and demonic. Although these factions have long existed in the American Jewish community, the polarization has reached a new level of intensity. It has gotten to the point where the far-left Jews identify more with the Palestinians than with the orthodox community and Israeli-Americans, and the right-leaning Jews have more in common with the evangelical Christians and the alt-right than with the liberal members of the American Jewish community! Strange days indeed!

With the election of Donald Trump, we are in a time of unpredictable and rapid changes in the United States. The Jewish community must observe this constantly evolving phenomenon with open eyes and a broad perspective—not with wishful thinking and indulgence in hatred for our political opponents. Otherwise, I fear, we will all be brought down together, regardless of our views on Trump, Israel, and whether Jewish values lie more legitimately on the left or right side of the political spectrum.

It seems that Richard Spencer and Steve Bannon have had their "15 minutes of fame" and have faded from public view. Spencer has returned to total obscurity, and since Bannon was fired in August 2017 from his position as White House chief strategist, he has not been visible in the Trump administration. He has, however, tried to promote his nationalist ideas on an international level and build a broader movement. But I wouldn't be so quick to dismiss the alt-right movement upon which Spencer and Bannon managed to bestow a small dose of legitimacy. There are indicators that American white supremacism continues to gain momentum. COVID-19 might be just the catalyst needed to bring it into the mainstream of U.S. political discourse.

COVID-19's devastation of the American economy has the potential to stir the white supremacist pot significantly and empower extreme nationalist movements who will portray the coronavirus as a devastating example of how America is under attack from "outside forces" who are trying to destroy it. This characterization will be extended to any group that is seen as over-encouraging international cooperation on combatting the virus or as denigrating Trump's efforts to reopen America and return it to the prosperity lost since the coronavirus shutdown.

The upcoming election will intensify the level of partisan rhetoric and attacks, and will spawn new conspiracy theories to provide a frightened American citizenry with identifiable "enemies" to blame for this health and economic disaster. In the middle ages the Jews were often blamed for plagues, accused of "poisoning the wells" or other dastardly deeds. I haven't heard COVID-19 portrayed as part of an international Jewish plot to take over the world, but I am sure this "formulation" is out there. Depressed economies remain optimal conditions for the growth of anti-Semitism and other hate-fueled popular movements.

Chapter 5
Zio-nationalism Part 3

Ilhan Omar Rekindles the Question of Dual-Loyalty Among American Zionists

Can American Zionists also be American patriots? This issue once again became front-page news. The revitalization of American nationalism, the growing radicalization of the Democratic Party, and the election of two outspoken Muslim congresswomen have brought this long-simmering question to the fore. Is there a divided loyalty among Americans who profess to be strong Zionist? In the not too distant past, much of the American Jewish leadership was passionately opposed to the establishment of a Jewish homeland, fearing it would create a perception that American Jews were less than fully American and lacking in loyalty to the United States. Shortly before the First Zionist Congress in Basel, the Union of American Hebrew Congregations (UAHC) declared:

> We are unalterably opposed to political Zionism. The Jews are not a nation, but a religious community. America is our Zion. Here, in the home of religious liberty, we have aided in founding a new Zion.

The Holocaust changed the calculus of the American Jewish fear that a Jewish homeland would expose Jews to suspicions of disloyalty. But with 75 years having passed since the end of the Holocaust, and the new juggernaut of American and worldwide nationalism on the right and radicalization on the left, this same issue has re-emerged with a vengeance. The Holocaust and its unprecedented horrors created a historical "vaccine" preventing the Western countries from propounding anti-Semitic perspectives and allowing world Jewry the "indulgence" of creating its own land to mitigate against the genocide of a third of their people and the insecurity and vulnerability that, it was understood, they felt in its aftermath. But as the Holocaust memory fades from the world and Israel has become a powerful, successful country, there is a new realignment of political forces. Israel and the American Jews are no longer "immune" from dual-loyalty suspicions and attacks.

The "Holocaust vaccine" that immunized the American Jewish community's support of Israel has worn off. Now American Jews will, I suspect, have to explain how their devotion to the State of Israel does not preclude or diminish their loyalty to the United States. The Jewish community, whether orthodox, conservative, reform, unaffiliated, or secular, in order to be "embraced" by the nationalist leadership of America and those anti-Israel elements on the left, will eventually need to make it clear that America comes first. If, for example, a nuclear deal or some international trade agreement is considered by nationalist-leaning Americans to be good for America, but bad for Israel, the American Jewish community will be expected to support such an agreement or deal.

As much as President Trump and his loyal followers may support what they see as Israel's nationalist prerogative to protect itself against its enemies, they will absolutely not support American Jews favoring Israel over what it views as best for the United States of America. Of course, the Jewish community leadership hopes and works to advance policies and situations that are mutually beneficial to both countries, and to my mind this is the current situation. A strong Israel is very good for American interests. But if a choice needs to be made, the American Jewish community will be expected to side with America in all things.

This nationalist perspective was famously expressed by President Theodore Roosevelt when he described the status of American immigrants. I believe it applies quite well to the issue we are discussing. He stated:

> In the first place, we should insist that if the immigrant who comes here in good faith becomes an American and assimilates himself to us, he shall be treated on an exact equality with everyone else, for it is an outrage to discriminate against any such man because of creed, or birthplace, or origin. But this is predicated upon the person's becoming in every facet an American, and nothing but an American.... There can be no divided allegiance here. Any man who says he is an American, but something else also, isn't an American at all. We have room for but one flag, the American flag.... We have room for but one language here, and that is the English language...and we have room for but one sole loyalty and that is a loyalty to the American people.

Nationalism's Impact on Anti-Zionists on the Right and Left

In 2015, during the heated process of the Obama administration's push to get the Iranian nuclear deal passed, it was Obama and the left, and not the right, that implied that the American Jewish community representatives were choosing Israel over the good of America. In an article in the *Washington Free Beacon* titled "White

House, Allies Accuse Jewish Lawmakers of Dual Loyalty to Israel" Adam Kredo wrote:

> The use of this rhetoric by the Obama administration and its allies is attracting concern among Jewish leaders, who worry the White House will pin the potential failure of the Iran deal on the American Jewish community. In a July 21 interview, Obama said that shady "lobbyists" and people with "money" were working to kill the deal. "I guarantee you, if people feel strongly about making sure that Iran doesn't get a nuclear weapon, without us going to war, and that is expressed to Congress, then people will believe in that," Obama told former Daily Show host Jon Stewart. "And the same is true on every single issue. If people are engaged, eventually the political system responds. Despite the money, despite the lobbyists, it still responds." Jewish publications questioned Obama's rhetoric, with some accusing the president of using anti-Semitic "dog whistles," a move that prominent detractors of Israel celebrated. Obama engaged in similar rhetoric during a July 15th speech about the deal in which he urged people to support the agreement "not based on lobbying, but based on what's in the national interests of the United States of America."

It is not new that the Obama administration often parted ways with the supporters of Israel, despite claims that Obama was "the best friend Israel ever had." The left's love/hate relationship with Israel and its embracing of the "Palestinian plight" is one of the reasons that many strong Zionists have rejected the Democratic Party and embraced Trump and the nationalists. This questioning of the American Zionists' loyalties has taken a new turn with the recent statements of Congresswoman Iham Omar and the reaction of the Democratic and Republican party leadership.

Omar's Accusation of American Zionists' Dual Loyalty

Ilhan Omar is a member of the U.S. Congress from Minnesota. Ms. Omar has made a number of statements that are widely perceived as anti-Semitic, specifically with regard to accusing American Jews and their leadership of having a dual loyalty to

Israel and America, and that Jewish campaign contributions are responsible for the U.S. government's support of Israel. She has also made statements that are decisively anti-Israel.

In recent months Omar wrote that U.S. support of Israel was "all about the Benjamins baby" ("Benjamins" is a slang term for money—Benjamin Franklin is on the hundred-dollar bill). Shortly thereafter she said, "I want to talk about the political influence in this country that says its O.K. to push for allegiance to a foreign country." When confronted with criticism about this remark by fellow Democrat Nita Lowey she replied, "I should not be expected to have allegiance/pledge support to a foreign country in order to serve my country in Congress or serve on a committee." After significant pressure from her party leadership she recanted these remarks.

The Democratic leadership responded to the backlash against Omar with a resolution that passed the House of Representatives, 407 to 23, on March 7, 2019. This resolution was itself controversial as it did not name Congresswoman Omar or directly address her remarks. Its language was broadened to include condemnation against anti-Muslim bigotry and discrimination against minorities. This change from the original language was viewed by many as a dilution of its purpose and to be motivated by pushback from younger, "progressive" Democrats such as Alexandria Ocasio-Cortez. A number of Democrats and Republicans were not pleased. "Why are we unable to singularly condemn anti-Semitism?" asked Rep. Ted Deutch, D-Florida, in a speech from the House floor. Nancy Pelosi, the speaker of the House, stated she was "confident that her (Omar's) words were not based on any anti-Semitic attitude" and that Omar "didn't have a full appreciation" of the "cultural impact" of her words and their offensive historic connotations. J Street welcomed the resolution and urged lawmakers to pass it "immediately."

President Trump wasted no time and minced no words in decrying the resolution. He described the Democrats as the "anti-Israel party" and as "an anti-Jewish party." "I thought yesterday's vote by the House was a disgrace," Trump said. Speaking to a group of RNC donors at Mar-a-Lago on March 8, 2019, Trump told the crowd assembled, "The Democrats hate Jewish people," according to three people who were there. Trump went on to say "he didn't understand how anyone who's Jewish could vote for a Democrat these days."

There is no doubt that regarding Israel and Zionism, Donald Trump and the Republican Party have to be seen as stronger supporters than the current Democratic Party. The obvious weakness and lack of resolve in the resolution that was brought about by Omar's anti-Semitic comments dramatically reveals the shifting dynamics and diminished support of the current Democratic Party for the State of Israel. I doubt this episode will result in a Jewish stampede to the Republican Party, but it may give pause to many Jews and perhaps tip a few that are on the fence to fall to the right. Jews, whether fervent Zionist or not, are quite sensitive to having their patriotic loyalties questioned and then not vigorously defended by their Democratic leaders. This will not be forgotten or left out of the calculus in that moment of decision that takes place in the privacy of the voting box when the curtains are drawn. Advice to the Democratic leadership: Do not underestimate the insecurity of a Jewish person when it comes to the threat of anti-Semitism or the accusation of dual loyalty.

With the 2020 election soon upon us and a decisive movement to the left by the Democratic Party, we will have to see if the accusations of American Jewish community dual loyalty re-emerge. This possibility will be exacerbated by any actions of Israel regarding annexation of West Bank areas. This issue is certain to be a flashpoint between those on the left that are focused on Palestinian rights and their perception that Israel is violating those rights and those fervent Zionists in the American Jewish community who see these annexations as essential to Israel's long-term security.

Chapter 6
The Jewish Anti-Trump Majority and Pro-Trump Minority

The American Jewish community's embrace of modern liberalism is unmatched by any other U.S. group. Merriam-Webster dictionary defines liberalism as:

> a political philosophy based on belief in progress, the essential goodness of the human race, and the autonomy of the individual and standing for the protection of political and civil liberties; specifically: such a philosophy that considers government as a crucial instrument for amelioration of social inequities (such as those involving race, gender, or class)

Modern liberalism in the United States is characterized by the dimension of *social liberalism* that endorses a market economy and the expansion of civil and political rights and liberties, but differs in that it believes the legitimate role of the government includes addressing economic and social issues such as poverty, healthcare, and education and combines ideas of civil liberty and equality with support for social justice. The American modern liberal philosophy strongly endorses public spending on programs such as education, healthcare, and welfare and focuses on addressing inequality, voting rights for minorities, reproductive and other forms of women's rights, support for LGBT rights, and immigration reform. (Source: Hugo Helco, in *The Great Society and the High Tide of Liberalism*, 2005)

A 2013 Pew Research Center study found that 49% of Jews identified as liberals compared to 21% of the general population. The study found that 67% of Jews who identified themselves as being "Jews of no religion" identified as liberals. http://www.pewforum.org/2013/10/01/chapter-6-social-and-political-views/.

Related to this, Pew also found that 70% of Jews identified as Democrat and 78% of "Jews of no religion" identified as Democrats, compared to a U.S. general population level of 49%. Orthodox Jews according to the Pew Study displayed an opposite trend, with only 12% identifying as liberal and 36% as Democrats. Moving to more recent findings, an article in *The Forward*, "By the Numbers: 3 Key Takeaways from the Jewish Vote," stated regarding the 2016 U.S. presidential election that 71% of American Jews voted for Clinton and 24% for Trump. Here too Trump appeared to be somewhat favored only by the orthodox Jewish voters, while Clinton was heavily favored by just about every other Jewish demographic. http://forward.com/news/353914/by-the-numbers-3-key-takeaways-from- the-2016-jewish-vote/

There are approximately seven million Jewish people in the United States of which 10% are estimated to be orthodox Jews. This calculates to approximately 700,000 orthodox Jews in the U.S. and about 6.3 million Jews of all other demographics, the great majority being liberal or liberal leaning. I would estimate that approximately 75% of Jewish community financial support and political clout is in the Democratic/liberal area. These numbers may be skewed by another growing group of non-liberal American Jews: the Israeli-American population (Those born in Israel or whose parents were born there). This growing demographic is estimated to be as large as 900,000, although official estimates are much smaller (in the 200,000 range). How many of these are citizens who vote is also, to my knowledge, unknown. Israeli-Americans, it seems, may favor Republicans and President Trump as well, based on the strong support that Republicans and Donald Trump have for the State of Israel and the fact that the Democratic Party under President Obama was seen as being a less than dependable ally. The Israeli-American political profile can be somewhat discerned by drawing on the political reaction to the presidential election in Israel itself. In a *Jerusalem Post* article by David Wiessman, "What Do the People of Israel Think About President-Elect Trump?" he writes:

> The exit polls in Israel showed Donald Trump won by a decent margin of 65 points. So how are Israelis reacting to the US election results? From my own observations, it seems that the majority of Israelis are in favor of a Trump victory…. I was part of the campaign team led by Marc Zell and the campaign team out of the State of Florida, which was my last home of record before I made aliya. I was grateful that the campaign team in Florida sent me a Trump hat and shirt, which I wore throughout the general election. The responses I received while wearing the Trump gear was 95 percent positive, even after the election.

A more recent Jewish Telegraphic Agency article, "Israeli Americans Represent a Growing 'New Power' in the Jewish Diaspora," by Alex Traiman (December 3, 2018), identified a similar pattern:

> Estimates of Israelis in America vary widely—from about 200,000 to as many as a million. According to the U.S. Department of Homeland Security, some 250,000 Israelis acquired permanent residence in the United States between 1949

(when 98 Israelis left the infant state) to 2015 (which saw about 4,000 Israelis move stateside). But that number does not chart deaths or Israelis who moved back. The 2013 Pew Research Forum study on American Jews found a similar number: About 300,000 Jews in America were either born in Israel or born to an Israeli parent. In total, Pew found that first or second-generation Israelis account for about 5 percent of American Jews. Even the Israeli government produces two different numbers. Israel's Central Bureau of Statistics reports than a little more than 500,000 Israelis in total moved abroad from 1990 to 2014—and nearly 230,000 came back. But Israel's U.S. Embassy told JTA that between 750,000 and 1 million Israelis live in the country. Adam Milstein, chairman of the Israeli-American Council, an umbrella group for Israelis here, told JTA that includes 400,000 children born to an Israeli parent.
https://www.jta.org/2017/07/31/united-states/why-more-israelis-are-moving-to-the-us

It makes sense that Israelis and Israeli-Americans would react positively to President Trump's tough talk on ISIS, Iran, and Islamic extremism and his lack of any particular interest in "making nice" with the Palestinians. So, if we add the Israeli-Americans to the orthodox Jews of America as being more supportive of Trump and the Republicans, we find an interesting dynamic duo that stands in political and ideological opposition to the liberal/left majority of American Jewry. Even with the Israeli-Americans and orthodox numbers combined, the Trump-supporting Jews of America are probably no more than 20% of the American Jewish population.

Why Are American Jews So Liberal?
To back up a bit, let us briefly draw on the insightful analysis of Dennis Prager's "Explaining Jews" series of articles to get a thumbnail sketch of why American Jews are so liberal. He cites six major reasons. Here they are, in his own words, slightly abbreviated:

1-Judaism is preoccupied with social justice (as well as with holiness and personal morality), and many Jews believe that the only way to achieve a just society is through leftist policies.

2-More than any other major religion, Judaism has always been preoccupied with this world. The (secular) Encyclopedia Judaica begins its entry on "Afterlife" by noting that "Judaism has always affirmed belief in an afterlife." But the preoccupation of Judaism has been making this world a better place.

3-Most Jews are frightened by anything that connotes right wing—such as the words "right-wing" and "conservative." Especially since the Holocaust, they think that threats to their security emanate from the Right only…nearly everyone regards the Nazis as far Right, and, therefore, Jews fear the Right. The fact that the Jews' best friends today are conservatives and the fact that the Left is the home of most of the Jews' enemies outside of the Muslim world have made little impact on Jews' psyches.

4-Liberal Jews fear most religion. They identify religion—especially fundamentalist religion and especially Christianity—with anti-Semitism. Jews are taught from birth about the horrors of the Holocaust, and of nearly 2,000 years of European, meaning Christian, anti-Semitism. They therefore tend to fear Christianity and believe that secularism guarantees their physical security. That is what animates the ACLU and its disproportionately Jewish membership, under the guise of concern with the Constitution and "separation of church and state" (words that do not appear in the Constitution), to fight all public expressions of Christianity in America.

5-Despite their secularism, Jews may be the most religious ethnic group in the world. The problem is that their religion is rarely Judaism; rather it is every "ism" of the Left. These include liberalism, socialism, feminism, Marxism and environmentalism.

Jews involved in these movements believe in them with the same ideological fervor and same suspension of critical reason with which many religious people believe in their religion. It is therefore usually as hard to shake a liberal Jew's belief in the Left and in the Democratic Party as it is to shake an evangelical Christian's belief in Christianity.

6-Liberal Jews fear nationalism. The birth of nationalism in Europe planted the secular seeds of the Holocaust (religious seeds had been planted by some early and medieval Church teachings and reinforced by Martin Luther). European nationalists welcomed all national identities except the Jews'. That is a major reason so many Jews identify primarily as "world citizens"; they have contempt for nationalism and believe that strong national identities, even in America, will exclude them.

Anti-Liberalism Among Orthodox Jews and Israeli-Americans

In the next chapter I would like to explore the growing animosity between the left and the right in American Jewry and any movement from one camp to the other. Now that the right-leaning Jews are, to some degree, supporters of Trump and the liberal Jews continue to view him as a true villain, we have a powerful, emotionally charged issue that has resulted in unprecedented animus between these Jewish groups. This is primarily the result of a face-off between the Haredi/Modern Orthodox/Israeli/senior citizen demographics and most other American Jews (conservative, reform, unaffiliated, secular), but of course the dividing line is not so clear-cut.

When Trump and Netanyahu are seen as being on the same page, this has a chilling effect on liberal Jews who have, for the most part, supported Israel with their significant funds and political clout. But the intensification of disdain is not just moving from left to right. The right-leaning Jewish demographic has a growing and intensifying loathing for the liberal position. As the extreme left has embraced the Palestinian cause with such fervor, the Palestinian-black unity has increased, and as the liberal position has moved to embrace the extension of marriage rights to homosexuals and transgender groups, the progressives are viewed more and more as the enemy of the religious and/or fervently Zionist American Jews. We have an ugly situation that can have profound negative ramifications for the American Jewish community and Israel. The Ilhan Omar debacle and the tepid response by the Democratic Party leadership has laid bare the radicalization of a significant part of the Democrats with its socialist leanings, Palestinian support, and liberation ideology. This has created some unprecedented "cracks" in the Jewish liberal wall with some lifelong Jewish Democrats considering jumping ship. Are we at a historic tipping point?

The COVID-19 pandemic has been sucking up all the oxygen due to its health and economic impact. This situation has perhaps created the illusion that this growing right/left conflict among Jews and the general population has lost some of its intensity. Once the pandemic has passed and things are "back to normal" these temporarily suspended political battles will return to the fore with renewed intensity and a desire to make up for lost time. The question remains whether this return will be in time for the November elections and how the COVID-19 pause will impact the form of the conflict upon its return.

Chapter 7
Schiff and Nadler:
Dynamic Duo of Anti-Trumpism

There are currently 24 Jewish members of the U.S. House of Representatives. Of these, 22 are Democrats and two are Republicans. There are also eight Jewish members of the U.S. Senate, all of which are Democrats. So, 30/32 of the Jewish members of Congress are Democrats—about 94% of all Jewish Congress members. The overwhelmingly Democratic and liberal nature of Jewish members of Congress is sometimes overlooked or minimized by those from demographics where Jews are highly supportive of Trump and the Republican Party. In addition, two leading Jewish Democratic congressmen, Adam Schiff and Jerry Nadler, head committees that strongly implicated President Trump's guilt during the two-year Mueller collusion investigation period and were at the forefront of the impeachment effort. (Schiff leads the House Intelligence Committee and Nadler leads the House Judiciary Committee).

William Barr, the Trump-appointed U.S. attorney general, provided a four-page summary to Congress of the Mueller Report findings, stating that no collusion (with Russia or anyone else) was found to have taken place during the 2016 presidential election, and that Mueller did not recommend the indictment of the president or any of his family or staff. Congressmen Schiff and Nadler, as chairs of their congressional committees, continued investigations into President Trump's activities leading up to his election in order to assess whether any activities had taken place that were either not discovered by the Mueller investigation or that raised concerns or risks, even though Mueller had decided they did not rise to the level of being indictable crimes. The House Judiciary Committee voted along party lines on April 3, 2019, to authorize the chairman to issue subpoenas for the full special counsel report and underlying materials, setting the stage for a potential legal battle between congressional Democrats and the Trump administration. Twenty-four Democratic committee members voted to authorize subpoenas for the full Mueller Report and the release of the underlying evidence to Congress. Seventeen Republicans voted no.

Schiff and Nadler spearheaded the intensive congressional investigations that led to the impeachment of President Trump. It is also interesting to note that in the U.S. Senate, the ranking Democratic member of the Senate Finance Committee is Senator Ron Wyden, who is Jewish (D-Oregon), and the ranking Democratic member of the Senate Judiciary Committee is Senator Diane Feinstein (D-California), who is also Jewish and one of Trump's most vociferous critics. In my opinion, the only reason these senators didn't carry out continuing investigations into Trump, post-Mueller and impeachment, is that the Senate is controlled by the Republicans. Lindsay Graham (R-South Carolina) chairs the Judiciary Committee and Chuck Grassley (R-

Iowa) chairs the Senate Finance Committee. If the Senate were controlled by the Democrats, it seems to me that Senate investigations into Trump would also be led by Jewish congressional members. These are not good optics for American Jews.

Don't misunderstand my position. I am not implying that Jewish Congress members are against Trump because they are Jewish. Almost all Democrats, Jewish or not Jewish, can be characterized as deeply anti-Trump and the more liberal, the more anti-Trump. Since the Jewish Americans and Jewish members of Congress are, for the most part, quite liberal, they are particularly anti-Trump as well. The liberal members of Congress who are not Jewish do not show any less "anti-Trumpness" than their Jewish colleagues. It is simply the overwhelmingly Democratic and liberal nature of the Jewish members of Congress that create this "Jewish connection." Even so, these Jewish congressional leaders being so prominently featured at the forefront of the ongoing attack on the Trump presidency is troubling.

This situation is viewed by Trump and his supporters as showing a lack of appreciation for all he has done for the Jewish community. Regardless of whether his motives are ideological or politically expedient, Trump is almost singlehandedly leading the U.S. government's unprecedented support of Israel (moving the U.S. Embassy to Jerusalem, cutting off funding to the Palestinians for paying stipends to terrorists, disengaging from the Iranian nuclear agreement, recognizing the Golan Heights and not pushing back against West Bank annexation efforts). He also has exceptionally close connections with the American Jewish community in numerous other ways (his utilizing of Jared

Kushner, an orthodox Jew, as his most trusted advisor, his being the grandfather to Jewish grandchildren, the numerous Jewish members he has selected for his cabinet, etc.). It very likely appears to those who are quite enamored and protective of President Trump (the fabled "Trump base") that there is a profound ingratitude by the American Jewish leadership and the majority of Jewish Americans who are so liberal toward a president who perceives himself, and is perceived by his strong supporters, as being the Jewish people's most faithful ally.

In this context, something else is quite disturbing. President Trump is perhaps the world's greatest rabble-rouser. Among the most disturbing phenomena of the Trump presidency are those raucous rallies he regularly holds in which he basks in the hate-tinged adoration of his followers. At these frequent gatherings, usually held in large arenas in deep red states and attended by dyed-in-the-wool "Trumpers," we see perhaps the darkest side of the Trump presidency. Trump whips the audiences into a frenzy against those that he identifies as his foes, or as the enemies of his base. Some of the most frequent targets are illegal immigrants, the "fake news" press, the impeachment, and of course the Democratic opposition.

At one of these rallies, President Trump targeted Representative Adam Schiff. At his "Make America Great Again" rally in Grand Rapids, Michigan, on March 28, 2019, the president called the chairman of the House Intelligence Committee "little pencil-neck Adam Schiff." "Many, many people were badly hurt by this scam," Trump said about the Mueller investigation "But more importantly, our country was hurt. Our country was hurt. And they are on artificial respirators right now. They are getting mouth-to-mouth resuscitation…. Little pencil-neck Adam Schiff. He's got the smallest, thinnest neck I've ever seen," the president said. "He is not a long-ball hitter, but I saw him today. 'Well, we don't really know, there still could have been some Russia collusion….' Sick, sick. These are sick people and there has to be accountability because it is all lies and they know it's lies."

At this first rally since the conclusion of special counsel Robert Mueller's investigation Trump also stated, "The Democrats have to now decide whether they will continue defrauding the public with ridiculous bull****, partisan investigations, or whether they will apologize to the American people."

Jewish Democratic members of the House of Representatives and the Senate have achieved significant positions of power and influence, leading their committees and having high-profile roles. These Congress members are also, almost exclusively, liberal (although perhaps not quite as far left as the new group of congressmen and congresswomen who took office in the midterm elections). This situation has put Jewish congressional leaders at the forefront of the battle against Trump and the effort, it seems, to rid the country of a president they judge to be incompetent, immoral, and simply unfit. The effort took on higher voltage with the impeachment, also led by Schiff and Nadler. The current COVID-19 situation has only exacerbated the situation, with Democrats placing blame for the high infection numbers and death toll on the Trump administration's ineffective response to the emergency.

For those who view this situation superficially, it might seem like all American Jews hate Donald Trump in spite of all the help and assistance that he has provided for Israel and the Jewish community. The truth is of course more nuanced, and many are appreciative of Trump's unambiguous support of the Jewish state, not to mention his boosting of the economy in the pre-COVID-19 period, his tough policy on Iran, and his decreasing of their taxes. But the truth remains that prominent Jewish congressional leaders are doing everything within their considerable power to bring down the Trump presidency regardless of his philo-Semitism. Although all but two congressional Democrats (over 90% of whom were not Jewish) voted for the impeachment inquiry, I suspect that there is a high correlation in the minds of many Trump supporters between the Jewish congressional leadership and the push to impeach POTUS 45 and remove him from office.

Chapter 8
Democrats Spurn AIPAC While
Republican Zionism Endures

This chapter will continue to explore the extreme level of disdain many orthodox and fervently Zionistic demographics of the American Jewish community have for their liberal brethren and vice-versa. All the elements are lined up in the current political climate to exacerbate a discord that has long existed between left- and right-leaning Jews. In the past the two camps have come together to support Israel, fight anti-Semitism, and promote other Jewish causes, providing common ground and a working relationship. But this détente is evaporating rapidly.

We will see that the right-leaning Jews' loathing of liberals (and vice-versa) has risen to an almost warlike level, with each group viewing the other as "the enemy." The right-wing Zionist camp has joined with many in the Trump camp that view the "mainstream media" as a mouthpiece and tool of liberal politics, especially with regards to the Israeli-Palestinian conflict and the legitimacy of the Donald Trump presidency. The liberal Jews, on the other hand, see Fox News as being little more than a Trump administration mouthpiece.

The Christian right (many, such as Secretary of State Mike Pompeo, who are in the Trump government) have become the greatest ally of the Zio-nationalists in America and have become the "wind beneath the wings" of right-leaning, Zionist, American Jews and their agenda to strengthen Israel. There is a strong religious dimension to the Christian right's support, recently expressed by Pompeo. He is a deacon at his evangelical church and fervent in his faith. As CNN reported on March 23, 2019:

> In an interview in Jerusalem, the Christian Broadcast Network's Chris Mitchell asked Pompeo, "Could it be that President Trump right now has been sort of raised for such a time as this, just like Queen Esther, to help save the Jewish people from the Iranian menace?" Esther is the main heroine of the Jewish holiday of Purim, which was celebrated this week. "As a Christian, I certainly believe that's possible," Pompeo said. Pompeo added that he is "confident that the Lord is at work here" when he sees the "remarkable history of the faith in this place and the work that our administration's done to make sure that this democracy in the Middle East, that this Jewish state, remains."

For many Jews this connection of the current political process to the Purim story was bolstered by the unexpected and unprecedented announcement by President Trump on Thursday, March 21, 2019 (Purim Day), that it was time for the United States to recognize the Golan Heights as part of sovereign Israel. Trump signed the order recognizing Israel's sovereignty over the Golan Heights when he met Prime Minister Netanyahu in Washington on Monday March 24, 2019. The prime minister was in town, in part, to address the 18,000-person annual AIPAC (America Israel Public Affairs Committee) convention.

AIPAC Democratic Presidential Candidate No-Shows
The 2019 AIPAC convention was quite telling in that many of the progressive Democratic presidential hopefuls skipped the event.

As the *New York Times'* Sheryl Gay Stolberg reported on March 23, 2019:

> But this year's confab is playing out in a changed and charged Washington political environment. Mr. Trump and his fellow Republicans have spent weeks lobbing accusations of anti-Semitism at Democrats, although the party remains the home of the vast majority of American Jews. And Democrats are under mounting pressure from their left flank to distance themselves from Aipac, which aligns itself closely with Mr. Netanyahu's far-right policies. A string of Democratic presidential candidates— Senators Bernie Sanders of Vermont, Elizabeth Warren of Massachusetts and Kamala Harris of California, as well as Beto O'Rourke and Julián Castro, among others—are skipping the conference. A group of freshman Democrats in the House, Ilhan Omar of Minnesota, Rashida Tlaib of Michigan and Alexandria Ocasio-Cortez of New York, has emerged as forthright critics of Israel and the United States' policy tilt toward the Israeli government. Those trends will stand in stark contrast to Mr. Trump's embrace of Mr. Netanyahu, who will meet the president for talks at the White House on Monday and at a dinner on Tuesday. "I don't know what happened to them, but they are totally anti-Israel," Mr. Trump said on Friday of the Democrats. "Frankly, I think they're anti-Jewish."

A March 22, 2019 *Jerusalem Post* article by Alon Einhorn noted on this issue:

> The absence of these Democratic candidates comes as the organization MoveOn called on the Democratic presidential candidates not to attend this year's conference, claiming that AIPAC worked to derail the nuclear agreement with Iran, on which former President Barack Obama worked hard, and on the grounds that the lobby uses "anti-Muslim and anti-Arab rhetoric." According to MoveOn, by boycotting the conference, Democratic candidates will be able to show that they are truly progressive.

The only candidate that explained his AIPAC absence from a policy disagreement perspective was Bernie Sanders. His senior adviser, Josh Orton, confirmed that Sanders did not attend and explained that Sanders "is very concerned about the stage that

AIPAC gives to leaders who have expressed extreme positions and who oppose the two-state solution." The other no-shows simply did not attend, without stating any criticism of Israel or Netanyahu.

The perspective of the right-leaning, Trump-supporting, fervently Zionist American Jew can be glimpsed from an article in the Front Page Magazine blog (frontpagemag.com) by David Greenfield titled, "The Jews That Choose Trump." This article stated:

> Many liberal Jews were traumatized when the racist hate group Black Lives Matter endorsed BDS. They fear being locked out of progressive politics. They are right to be afraid. UK Labor's purge of Jews is a sign of things to come. There is no future for Jews on the left except as collaborators in anti-Semitism. Mainstream Jewish liberals were shocked by Obama's embrace of anti-Semitic language in support of the Iran Deal. They were upset when Hillary Clinton and then Cory Booker backed the nuke sellout. To be a Jew on the left is to experience a constant stream of such betrayals and surprises. Remaining there will require confessing their Jewish privilege and apologizing for their very existence. But that is what they have been doing, in one form or another, all along. The FDR Jews chose the Democratic Party over the six million Jews who died in the Holocaust. Now the FDR Jew is passing into his last twilight. The irreconcilable contradictions of his existence are finally coming apart. The American Jewish community is slowly being divided. The center is vanishing. To remain on the left will require abandoning Israel and accepting anti-Semitism as normative. And there will be many Jews on the left who will happily make that terrible bargain. You can already see them protesting outside synagogues, harassing Jewish charities who donate to Israel and defending the career anti-Semites of the left. The rest will pay tribute to their ethnic origins by sharing "Top 5 Jewish Things About Hillary" listicles and marveling at her name clumsily spelled out in Hebrew letters.

Why support Hillary? Because she is less anti-Israel than Bernie Sanders. The characterization of the mindless absurdity of liberal Jews is a typical perspective of those Jews, orthodox, Israeli-American or otherwise, who stridently reject Jewish-American liberalism and, almost as strongly embrace Trump, the right and even the new American nationalism. Even former Breitbart editor and former White House adviser, Steve Bannon has got a following among the Right-leaning American Zionist Jews. This in spite of the many indications that Bannon is cozy with the Alt-Right movement, giving them their national forum on the Breitbart website. Mort Klein, the strongly right-leaning head of Zionist Organization of America (ZOA) wrote on its website:

> ZOA's own experience and analysis of Breitbart articles confirms Mr. Bannon's and Breitbart's friendship and fair-mindedness toward Israel and the Jewish people. To accuse Mr. Bannon and Breitbart of anti-Semitism is Orwellian. In fact, Breitbart bravely fights *against* anti-Semitism…. It is painful to see Anti-Defamation League (ADL) president Jonathan Greenblatt engaging in character assassination against President-elect Trump's appointee Stephen Bannon and Mr. Bannon's company, Breitbart Media. ADL/Greenblatt essentially accused Mr. Bannon and his media company of "anti-Semitism" and Israel hatred, when Jonathan Greenblatt/ADL tweeted that Bannon "presided over the premier website of the 'alt right'–a loose knit group of white nationalists and anti-Semites."
> http://zoa.org/2016/11/10342353zoacriticizesadlforfalselyalleg ingtrumpadvisorbannonis antisemitic

The left-leaning Jewish newspaper *Forward* stated in the provocatively titled article "The Breathtaking Hypocrisy of Jews Who Line Up with Steve Bannon's Twisted Vision of America":

> So obsessed are we with looking for threats from one direction that we have missed the growing danger from another. Unleashed by Donald Trump's presidential campaign and cemented by the appointment of Stephen Bannon to a powerful position in the White House, the anti-Semitic sentiments of the far right are closer to the center of political power than they have been in recent memory. Bannon may be, as Klein insisted, "the opposite of an anti-Semite," but the news organization he oversaw until he joined the Trump campaign unabashedly embraced the white supremacist movement that is anti- immigrant, anti-feminist, anti-Muslim—and at times, anti-Semitic. "We're the platform for the alt-right," Bannon proudly told Mother Jones last summer. Some of those pro-Trump alt-right guys are the ones sending horrific anti-Semitic messages laden with Holocaust imagery to Jewish journalists—and others around the country. As our Naomi Zeveloff explained earlier this week, it's possible to be Zionist

and anti-Semitic at the same time. Some, like Bannon, see in Israel a (white) nationalist, anti-Arab country worth supporting—over there. Here, in America, they may accept, even respect, individual Jews, but their ideological aim is to cleanse the country of its multiculturalism and restore privilege to white Christian males.

http://forward.com/opinion/354569/thebreathtakinghypoc risyofjewswholineupbehindstevebannonstwisted/

Steve Bannon, though not in the same spotlight as he was a year or two ago, is still a pivotal point of divergence for the profoundly bifurcated American Jewish community. He is the opposite of a liberal, rejecting universalism for a strident nationalism and all the exclusionary elements that it entails. On the other hand, he may embrace the Israeli right's cause, which supports its own strong nationalist agenda to protect itself from its foes and putting its country and its people first. If an American Jew is a fervent Zionist with nationalist sympathies, he or she seems to be able to overlook the unseemly and possibly dangerous elements of Bannon's approach. But for liberals who are already conflicted about Netanyahu and his coalition putting a strong, secure Israel first and its taking measures that the UN and the left perceive as harsh and unjust, the aligning of these policies with the likes of President Trump and Steve Bannon intensifies the internal conflict to a dizzying level.

The American Jewish community is in a war with itself, which has been simmering for a long time. It has now been brought into the open with the election of Donald Trump. Jewish Liberalism vs. Zionist Nationalism is the core issue of this *kulturkampf.* Who will win? I fear it will be neither. In this regard, the recent article "The Great Jewish Divide: Jews Have Stopped Talking to their Fellow Jews; What It Means for America, Israel and our Jewish Community" by Steven Windmueller, PhD, on behalf of the Wind Group, Consulting for the Jewish Future, states:

Little today binds America's Jews together. Can we even be defined at this point as a community? "Community" implies a set of shared values and common goals. But is there anything that aligns these divergent factions? The underlying question is whether such deeply entrenched political divisions create a problem for our community to achieve its long-term interests? Friendships have ended over political disagreements, and organizations have been pressured to "take positions" as these battle lines intensify and sharpen. As I have written elsewhere, "Civility and consensus have given way to name-calling and political separation."

This deepening divide has many ramifications for American Jewry and for America, as Jewish economic and political power will, in many ways, neutralize each other's effectiveness in this pitch battle for the soul and direction of the American Jewish community.

Jewish Division on the West Bank Annexation

The intention of the new Netanyahu/Ganz government to annex those areas of the West Bank with Israeli settlement (approximately 30% of the land) is sure to intensify the Jewish division on Trump Israeli policy. The Trump administration is supportive of the move, as opposed to Europe, the Arab countries, and most of the international community. A May 13,

2020 article on bloomberg.com titled "Now That He Can Annex West Bank Land, Will Netanyahu Do It?" By Gwen Ackerman, Ivan Levingston, and Fadwa Hodali states:

Israeli Prime Minister Benjamin Netanyahu has been promising for more than a year to annex West Bank land the Palestinians want for a state. With Donald Trump in the White House, he's now got the backing he needs to turn that pipedream of the Israeli right and nightmare of the Palestinians into reality. The economic carnage of the coronavirus has cast a shadow on Trump's re-election prospects, however, and Netanyahu has to move fast if he wants to be assured of getting this done under the aegis of the U.S. president's Middle East peace plan.... Netanyahu has said he'd like to extend Israeli sovereignty over all of the roughly 130 heavily fortified settlements, dozens of satellite outposts, and "other areas important to our security, our heritage, and our future." Under the Trump plan, that would account for about 30% of the West Bank, leaving the Palestinians with non-contiguous enclaves that would be joined by a system of tunnels and bridges…The U.S. will support it, but the European Union, some Gulf Arab states, and presumptive U.S. Democratic presidential nominee Joe Biden have already spoken out against it. "Annexation will not pass unnoticed or, if it proceeds, there will be a reaction," EU foreign-policy spokesman Peter Stano told reporters in Brussels on May 11. Several member states seek the threat of sanctions to deter annexation, including possibly denying Israel membership in trade agreements, special grants or cooperative ventures, Israel's Haaretz daily reported. But EU foreign-policy chief Josep Borrell said the EU is "far away" from weighing any sanctions on Israel, while acknowledging the plan is "very divisive" within the bloc.

It is safe to say that a Democratic administration under Joe Biden or any other Democratic president would not support this plan. This puts pressure on the Netanyahu/Ganz to do whatever it intends to do before the 2020 U.S. presidential elections. Those Jewish organizations on the left of the spectrum have already expressed their opposition. The Union of Reform Judaism said in a statement:

> We call on this new government to refrain from unilateral actions that could potentially hinder or thwart the renewal of the peace process in the short and long term, especially unilateral annexation."

The Israeli-Policy Forum stated:

> We hope that the new Israeli government closely examines the potential consequences of unilateral annexation and the deleterious impact it will have on Israeli security and diplomacy and that it heeds the warnings against unilateral annexation that have come from Israeli security experts, the United States Congress, the European Union, foreign policy experts, and American Jewish leaders.

J Street said in a statement it was "deeply alarmed" by the language on annexation in the Netanyahu-Gantz agreement, and cautioned that it "would severely imperil Israel's future as a democratic homeland for the Jewish people, along with the future of the U.S.-Israel relationship." It urged "responsible American leaders" to express their stark opposition to annexing parts of the West Bank.

AIPAC, the leading lobby group supporting Israel in Washington, refrained from mentioning the matter of West Bank annexation in its official statement congratulating Netanyahu and Gantz for the formation of the new government. Neither have the Orthodox Union or the Agudath Israel organizations, which represent elements of the orthodox American Jewish community. Suffice it to say that this issue has just begun to make its impact on the Jewish community, and once the COVID-19 virus pandemic crisis has passed, it will become quite the rallying point for both the right and the left in the Jewish and general community.

Chapter 9
Will Democratic Progressivism Turn American Jewry to the Right?

The basic ratio is 3:1: Out of four American Jewish voters, three vote Democratic and one votes Republican (more or less). This is pretty much the "given" when it comes to the Jewish vote in presidential elections. I have read different statistics but for the Trump/Clinton campaign, as mentioned, it was about 26% for Trump and 74% for Clinton. In those states that are "deep blue," the outcome of the Jewish vote is inconsequential. For the "blood red" states, the Jewish vote is also of no meaningful impact. But let's look at those "purple states." Here the Jewish vote, though small in number, can potentially tip the balance. These are the states whose electoral votes made all the difference in electing Donald Trump president over the heavy favorite, Hillary Clinton, in 2016 and they are really the only ones that are in play in 2020. Here is a list of 13 purple or "swing" states, meaning that they have a recent history of voting for either Democrats or Republicans:

Arizona: 11 electoral votes. The state has voted for the Republican presidential nominee in 9 of the last 10 elections.

Colorado: 9 electoral votes. The state has voted for the Republican presidential nominee in 7 of the last 10 elections.

Florida: 29 electoral votes. The state has voted for the Republican presidential nominee in 6 of the last 10 elections.

Georgia: 16 electoral votes. The state has voted for the Republican presidential nominee in 7 of the last 10 elections.

Iowa: 6 electoral votes. The state has voted for the Democratic presidential nominee in 6 of the last 10 elections.

Michigan: 16 electoral votes. The state has voted for the Democratic presidential nominee in 6 of the last 10 elections.

Minnesota: 10 electoral votes. The state has voted for the Democratic presidential nominee in each of the last 10 elections (very small margin in 2016 election).

Nevada: 6 electoral votes. The state has voted for the Republican presidential nominee in 6 of the last 10 elections.

New Hampshire: 4 electoral votes. The state has split its vote between the Republican and Democratic presidential nominees in the past 10 elections.

North Carolina: 15 electoral votes. The state has voted for the Republican presidential nominee in 8 of the last 10 elections.

Ohio: 18 electoral votes. The state has split its vote between the Republican and Democratic presidential nominees in the past 10 elections.

Pennsylvania: 20 electoral votes. The state has voted for the Democratic presidential nominee in 7 of the last 10 elections.

Virginia: 13 electoral votes. The state has voted for the Republican presidential nominee in 8 of the last 10 elections.

Wisconsin: 10 electoral votes. The state has voted for the Democratic presidential nominee in 8 of the last 10 elections.

There is speculation that Texas may be entering the "purple zone" due to the closeness of the 2018 midterm Senate elections in which Ted Cruz defeated Beto O'Rourke by only 2.7%, whereas Trump beat Clinton by 9% in the presidential contest. If Texas goes purple it would significantly change the electoral map. The 166,505 Jews living in Texas are only 0.6% of the population, but still could have an impact in a very close race for Texas's 38 electoral votes.

The most consequential of the current purple states due to their high number of electoral votes are Florida (29 electoral votes), Pennsylvania (20 electoral votes), and Ohio (18 electoral votes). There is really no path to electability for a president without winning Florida. If a candidate can win Florida, Ohio, and Pennsylvania, he or she has basically won the election. In the 2016 election Trump won all three. The Jewish populations of these states as of 2018 were:

Florida: 629,120 (3% of the state population)
Ohio: 148,115 (1.3% of the state population)
Pennsylvania: 298,240 (2.3% of the state population)

Total Jewish population in these three states: 1,075,475

There are a little over a million "purple Jews" out of an estimated U.S. Jewish population of about seven million who live in these

major purple states. Since Jewish voter turnout is about 80%, about a third higher than the average voter turnout for the U.S., the Jewish voter impact is also a third higher than their numbers reflect. Let's look at the popular vote totals for these states in the 2016 presidential election:

Florida: Trump 4,617,886; Clinton 4,504,975
2016 Margin: Trump +112,911

Ohio: Trump 2,841,005; Clinton 2,394,164
2016 Margin: Trump +446,841

Pennsylvania: Trump 2,970,733; Clinton 2,926,441
2016 Margin: Trump +44,292

Based on these numbers, the Jews of Florida and Pennsylvania have the potential to be particularly consequential; their numbers are almost a million and the voter difference total between Trump and Clinton in 2016 was under 170,000 votes. Of course, not all of these million "purple Jews" are of voting age or vote, but Jewish population voter numbers in these states are still of potentially significant electoral importance. It is ironic that the larger Jewish populations in deep blue states, though they can successfully impact state and city elections, due to their large percentage, have almost no meaningful impact on the presidential election. Neither Trump, nor whoever becomes the Democratic presidential candidate, cares much how the Jewish population of New York, Massachusetts, or California vote. Though the Jewish populations of these states are large, the states will go Democratic regardless of how the Jews vote. It's the purple state Jews, like those in Florida and Pennsylvania, that are the focus of presidential candidates' interest and campaigning.

Will Jews Move Right or Left in 2020 Election?

Matt Brooks, the executive director of the Republican Jewish Coalition (RJC), said in a recent interview that the congressional representative Ilhan Omar controversy would help him make a case that he has pressed for a decade: that Democrats are not doing enough to combat anti-Israel and anti-Jewish activity within their ranks. "There is a virulent strain within the Democratic Party that's on the rise in terms of anti-Semitic and Israel bias," said Brooks, adding that the RJC is planning a massive get-out-the-vote drive among Jews ahead of the 2020 presidential election.

Former Trump campaign aid and model Elizabeth Pipko recently started "Jexodus" (a portmanteau of the two words "Jewish" and "exodus") to move Jewish Democratic voters to the Republican Party ahead of the upcoming presidential election, particularly in swing states where the Jewish vote can still make a difference (https://theexodusmovement.com/). Trump's recent tweet about Jexodus was a PR coup for the group. In a news release announcing its launch, Jexodus wrote:

> We are proud Jewish Millennials tired of living in bondage to leftist politics. We reject the hypocrisy, anti-Americanism, and anti-Semitism of the rising far-left. Progressives, Democrats, and far too many old-school Jewish organizations take our support for granted. After all, we're Jewish, and Jews vote for Democrats.

According to its website, the group is composed of, or designed to cater to, "young Jews who are disenchanted with the Democratic party." This imagined "move to the right" of the Jewish community is not at all the way those in the Jewish Democratic leadership see things. Democratic leaders have stated it is absurd to claim that Jews were leaving the party. The Jewish Democratic Council of America (JDCA) noted that Jewish votes for Democratic candidates actually increased in the November

midterms. "Republicans have lost support among Jewish voters since President Trump took office," JDCA said in a statement. "According to exit polling, support for Trump among the Jewish electorate in 2016 was 24 percent, while support for Republicans among Jewish voters in 2018 fell to 17 percent."

But this voting trend preceded the episode with Ilhan Omar and the accusations that the freshman Minnesota Democrat had used anti-Semitic rhetoric. Omar's said she felt pressured into "pledging allegiance" to Israel; Jews in the Democratic House charged that she was invoking an anti-Semitic slander of dual loyalty. That led to a resolution passed by the House that condemned anti-Semitism, Islamophobia, and other forms of hate. But many in the Jewish community saw it as a weak response to a stark act of anti-Semitism that required an unequivocal response.

There is also a growing comfort zone with some form of socialism in the Democratic platform that is new and untested with regards to how the Jewish voting public will react to it. If socialism and anti-Zionism become "intersectionally" linked to the new 2020 Democratic Party platform, it may give some pause to even the most dedicated Jewish liberal Democratic voters. One often doesn't know when "the tipping point" has been reached until well after it happens. Has the Democratic Party reached a tipping point for Jewish voters to "tip" Republican? Interestingly, in May 2020 presumptive Democratic presidential nominee Joe Biden and his chief primary rival, Senator Bernie Sanders, I-Vermont, announced the members of a joint task force meant to unify the party ahead of November's general election, bringing together figures from different wings of the party, which included New York Rep. Alexandria Ocasio-Cortez. Cortez represents, in the

opinion of many, the growing, empowered far left sector of the Democratic Party, which includes Ihan Omar among its more outspoken members.

How *Not* to Convert Liberal Democrats to the Republican Party

I called this book *Loving Trump, Hating Trump* in part because I have observed a deep emotional division in the Jewish community centered on President Trump. Some love him—they even love his bad manners, childish speech patterns, insults, lack of depth of knowledge about the issues, lying, etc. All of these are seen through the lens of the clever trickster using his innate brilliance to overturn a corrupt, self-loving, self-absorbed liberal establishment that is destroying everything. Some hate him—even when he clearly improves the economic conditions for millions of people, destroys ISIS, defends and supports Israel like no previous president, etc. They still utterly loath the man. In both cases, without delving into the psychology of these strong feelings, there is much more going on than just whether you are for or against Trump's policies. It's the man himself. People often adore people who hurt them and hate people who can help them.

My advice to Republican leaders and those who love Trump and want to move those who hate Trump to vote Republican is not to make it all about how wonderful President Trump is and that these former Democrats must "see the light" and come to appreciate how truly great this individual is. This will not happen. Maybe one in a thousand will have such a dramatic conversion. So how do you convince someone to vote for a person they loathe? Self-interest.

The history of politics is the history of people supporting those they don't personally like but who will help them achieve their goals. I can loath Trump and vote for him if he will make my life and the life of my family better, even if I much prefer the personal qualities and moral stance of the Democratic candidate. Only when voting Democratic is perceived as being contrary to the Jewish community's self-interest and security will it turn right. On the other hand, hating someone is also quite powerful and motivating, and the Jewish vote may just stay where it is, or even turn further to the left.

Chapter 10
Who Gets to Define Morality in Trump's America?

There is an ongoing battle raging in the United States among fierce combatants. The objective of each of the adversaries in this (so far) bloodless war, is to decide who gets to define the moral boundaries for America. Who defines what "good" looks like? Who has the privilege of determining which actions and statements are categorized as "evil"? Although scientific method has become the standard of establishing the true nature of the physical world (anti-vaxxers and flat-earthers not withstanding), morality in America or anywhere else has no such broadly agreed-upon test or method of verification.

This fight for moral dominance has been going on since America (and human civilization) began. But there are periods in a country's or civilization's history where the moral battles are particularly heated. This, I believe, is one of those times. With a secular worldview becoming more widespread, and the wholesale dismissal of previously held "moral truths" becoming the litmus test of progressivism, America finds itself in a shifting moral universe that is hot, swirling, and amorphous, yet to take solid form.

The Rapid Rise of Secularism

In an April 1, 2018 article by Michael Shermer in *Scientific American* titled "The Number of Americans with No Religious Affiliation Is Rising," he writes that "a 2015 Pew Research Center poll reported that 34-36% of Americans said they were affiliated with no religion." This compares to a rate of 16% of those not identifying with any religion in 2007 and an increase from 36.6 million to 55.8 million between 2007 and 2016. In a January 2018 article in the journal *Social Psychological and Personality Science* entitled "How Many Atheists Are There?," Will M. Gervais and Maxine B. Najle estimated that 26% (64 million) of Americans identify as atheists.

A Public Relations Research Institute (PRRI) survey in 2017 found that among those Jews under age 30, 57% defined themselves as Jews of no religion or "cultural Jews." The PEW 2013 study of American Jews found millennial Jews who categorize themselves as "no religion" comprised about 32% of that age group. In sharp contrast to these young American Jews, 78% of Jewish seniors (age 65 or older) identified as religiously Jewish, while 22% identified as culturally Jewish." These surveys indicate a dramatic shift toward a secular/cultural Jewishness among younger people, if there is any Jewishness at all.

But while secularism is in rapid ascendance, there has also been a strengthening of the impact and political clout of religious groups in America, which have made particularly significant gains during the Trump presidency. Evangelical Christians are now the largest Christian demographic in the country (25.4%), exceeding both the

Catholics and other Protestant denominations. They are also the Christian group with the most political influence. Their clout has been significantly increased with their backing of President Trump and his appointment of two conservative justices to the Supreme Court. These appointments have created a conservative majority on the court and put the overturning of *Roe v. Wade* and the federal right to an abortion back on the table, which is one of the most, if not *the* most, important issues for the Christian Right.

In the American Jewish population, the growth and influence of the Orthodox Jewish community has also increased, and they are, for the most part, in close agreement with the Evangelicals on a broad spectrum of political and "values" issues. This places American Orthodox Jews squarely at odds with their more liberal Jewish brethren from the conservative, reform, and unaffiliated sectors.

The Combatants

Here is my list of the major battle groups in the war for moral dominance in America:

1- **The Liberal Media** led by CNN, MSNBC, the *New York Times*, the *Washington Post, the Huffington Post and Slate.com* . These TV, online and print media giants are the first and last word for most liberal and secular Americans regarding which people, actions, and beliefs are moral and good and which are evil. They are truly the high priests and priestesses of secular-liberalism in the U.S. With hundreds of millions watching and absorbing the message, it is hard to underestimate the power of the liberal media in shaping what Americans believe to be right and wrong, good and bad, moral and immoral. Although the particular agendas of these media giants may differ, most embrace a secular, "compassionate" capitalism (those listed above are all billion-dollar profit-making businesses in spite of a continuous touting of concern for the poor and the disaffected). They are strident in their support of abortion rights, the empowerment of women in society, gay rights, "green" environmental policy, and expanding the legislative scope of moral issues such as bullying and hate, and for broadening the legal definition of discrimination. Regarding the COVID-19 pandemic, the liberal media has favored a cautious approach to reopening the economy and has portrayed the Trump administration as reckless and lacking judgment in what is portrayed as rushing the process of easing quarantine restrictions. This accelerated normalization of activities is seen as increasing the risk of higher mortality and a resurgence of the virus.

2- **The Conservative Media** led by Fox News and Breitbart News are powerful media mouthpieces for rightwing, conservative views. The *Wall Street Journal* is also decidedly conservative, especially regarding business and economic issues. Others of this ilk include *National Review*, *The Blaze* and *The Federalist*. However, even these news outlets have accepted much of the moral positions of the liberal news media, although perhaps in a less extreme manner. But they differ from them on a number of key issues including not being uniformly pro-abortion, having a strong pro-Zionist position, embracing "America First" nationalism, being more supportive of police and law and order, and embracing a less regulated free market. Although not monolithic on the point, the conservative media has supported Trump's push to reopen the economy in the wake of the COVID-19 outbreak. This disagreement on the pace of reopening business and recreational areas has come to reflect the right/left political splint of the country, with the right favoring reopening and the left recommending caution.

3-**The Christian Right**, which is made up primarily of the Evangelical Christians and the Roman Catholics. The Pew Research Center findings are that 70.6% of Americans identify as Christians. The core Christian Right are composed of the 25.4% of Americans who identify as Evangelical Christians and the 23.9% who identify as Catholics. The Evangelicals and Catholics are quite distinct in their economic views, and in their support of Israel, but they come together strongly in areas such as the opposition to abortion and gay marriage.

4-The American Far Left, which many have lumped together with American liberals, but who actually have quite a distinct character. The American Left, of which Senator Bernie Sanders may be considered the current leading light, has strong socialist leanings when compared to the decidedly capitalist views of liberals. Mark Zuckerburg and the others of the Silicon Valley billionaire set, as well as most wealthy movie and music stars, not to mention leading news media personalities, may be decidedly liberal, but they are certainly not American Left socialists.

The American far left also tends to view the United States and its economic/military complex as being a force of evil in the world. They disdain its support of policies and foreign leaders who they view as tools of the wealthy to maintain and expand their power. Most include the State of Israel under its current government as also being part of this sinister force, and of being persecutory toward the Palestinians, who the left supports and strongly sympathizes with as an oppressed group. They categorize Israel as another example of the powerful abusing the powerless.

A significant portion of American Jews belong to the American Left. A recent Pew Research survey seems to bear this out. This survey found 42% of American Jews think Trump is favoring the Israelis too much, while a similar share (47%) say he is striking the right balance between Israelis and Palestinians. The rest either say he is favoring the Palestinians too much (6%) or they don't know (4%). By comparison, Christians in the United States are more likely to say Trump is striking the right balance between the Israelis and Palestinians (59%) than to say Trump favors the Israelis too much (26%). Among Evangelical Protestants, 72% think Trump strikes the right balance between Israel and

Palestinians, and just 15% say Trump favors Israel too much. https://www.pewresearch.org/facttank/2019/05/06/u-s-jews-are-more-likely-than-christians-to-say-trump-favors-the-israelis-too-much/

The American Left, unlike American liberals, does not particularly embrace the Jewish people, which it views as too rich, too empowered, and too privileged to be a legitimate moral compass. The Holocaust was long ago, along with those poor Jews who struggled against poverty and persecution to achieve success in America. Although there are many Jews who identify with the American Left, their Judaism and Jewish roots are viewed primarily by the Left as negatives. Other groups have taken the lead as the vanguard and visionaries of the Left. These groups, due to their being viewed as victims and their relative lack of wealth and power in America, are considered to possess greater moral clarity. They include the black and Hispanic communities, the American Muslim community, and those who are gay or transgender. Although I would agree that wealth and power are significant impediments to moral clarity, a lack of power and wealth does not, in itself, result in any sharpening of one's sense of justice.

The Jewish people have long been a factor in shaping moral positions in society. But this was not due to the persecutions of exile alone. The Jewish people had and have the tradition of the Torah and its moral teaching, which, along with its long experiencing the cruel treatment of the powerful, resulted in a particular passion for justice and mercy. Failure to thrive in itself does not a prophet make, and usually has the opposite effect—to fill an individual or group with rage, which distorts their thinking about moral issues.

4-The Democratic Congress, though composed of a somewhat conflicted combination of liberal and left politicians, has emerged as a key player in the battle for moral dominance. At the liberal forefront presently, we find two Jewish congressmen, Jerry Nadler, the chairman of the House Justice Committee, and Adam Schiff, the chairman of the House Intelligence Committee. Both are focused on discovering misdeeds by the president and his "minions" and are continuing to present themselves as the voices of justice and truth, battling a corrupt, dishonest commander in chief and a feckless, cowardly Republican-led Senate. These two figures were also at the center of the impeachment of the president.

5-President Trump is perhaps the most potent player in the current battle for moral leadership. Although the latest polls consistently show a 40-45% approval rating range for the president, this does not mean that his impact and influence is limited to this minority of Americans. It's like advertising. Everybody thinks they are not affected by it, but everyone is. In part, it's this thinking that you're immune that makes you more vulnerable to being affected. With the power of his Twitter account, which has over 60 million followers, his speeches and rallies, not to mention the endless press, both positive and negative, which reports on his every word and deed, President Trump is, for better or worse, by far the most powerful voice for just what constitutes morality in the United States of America today.

Chapter 11

Varieties of American Anti-Semitic Experiences

It is disturbing to reflect on the variety and intensity of hatred that is seething in the United States today. The official "out-lawing" of hate by recent statutes and regulations has had little actual effect on the prevalence of this most base and basic of human emotions. Endless television and online media continuously display the deep loathing between those on the left and those on the right, as well as between the devoutly secular and the devoutly religious.

At times this vitriol is presented in an intellectual, civil manner, and at other times, in a display of basic, raw hatred. Sporadically, it has resulted in violence and deadly attacks. As with all things these days, President Trump seems to be at the epicenter of the erupting "hatequake." Although the Jews are certainly not the only focus of this growing hatred, they are, as they have often been, a most popular target for a diverse group of factions that despise them, for a variety of reasons.

What are these different flavors of Jew-hatred and what are the potential negative outcomes for the Jewish community? And just what is President Trump's role in the recent rise in American anti-Semitism, with his unique constellation of qualities including: unprecedented support for the State of Israel, an appearance of sympathy with white nationalists, a heavy reliance on Jews in his cabinet, as well as having an Orthodox Jewish daughter and grandchildren.

The three major categories of contemporary American anti-Semitism, as I see them are:

1- Hatred of the Jews by white supremacist-leaning individuals and other groups who blame Jews for the liberal policies of America, particularly in the area of immigration and civil rights legislation. The October 2018 massacre at the Tree of Life synagogue in Pittsburgh and the more recent one at Chabad of Poway fall into this category. The annual survey by the Center for Southern Poverty published in 2019 found the number of hate groups reaching a record high of 1,024, up from 784 four years earlier with a 7% rise from 2017 to 2018. The most significant growth was in the number of white nationalist organizations, up from 100 in 2017 to 148 in 2018.
https://www.usatoday.com/story/news/nation/2019/02/20/hate-groups-white-power-supremacists-southern-poverty-law-center/2918416002/)

2- Hatred of Israel and Zionist American Jews by the left and by those Muslim Americans who have demonized Israel as an aggressive, imperialist force and an apartheid state that has robbed the Palestinians of their land and their freedom. This group includes the BDS (Boycott, Divest, Sanctions) movement and its supporters, many of whose groups are active on college campuses.

Israel has banned these groups from entering the country:
The list includes:

· AFSC (American Friends Service Committee)
· AMP (American Muslims for Palestine)
· American Friends Service Committee
· Code Pink
· JVP (Jewish Voice for Peace)
· NSJP (National Students for Justice in Palestine)
· USCPR (U.S. Campaign for Palestinian Rights)
· BNC (BDS National Committee)

Additional Palestinian-rights Jewish organizations include:

· Jews for Palestinian Right of Return
· Jews of Color and Sephardi and Mizrahi
· Jews in Solidarity/Palestine
· Jews Say No!

Statements by these groups, whether Jewish or not, object vociferously to the idea that their anti-Zionism is a form of anti-Semitism. A letter signed in July 2018 by 36 BDS supporting groups stated:

> As social justice organizations from around the world, we write this letter with growing alarm regarding the targeting of organizations that support Palestinian rights in general and the nonviolent Boycott, Divestment and Sanctions (BDS) movement, in particular. These attacks too often take the form of cynical and false accusations of anti-Semitism that dangerously conflate anti-Jewish racism with opposition to Israel's policies and system of occupation and apartheid.
> https://www.maccabeetaskforce.org/far-left-jewish-groups-defend-israel-critics-from-false-accusations-of-anti-semitism/

3- Hatred of the Jews due to their financial prowess and what is perennially perceived as a conspiratorial manipulation of markets and business to enrich themselves at the expense of those who work hard but struggle financially. This group of haters comes in many varieties—black, white, rich, poor, etc. I also believe that this form of anti-Semitism has the widest diversity of degrees— from the person who has a mildly, suspicious disdain for "Jews and their money" to those who view Jews as a demonic, international conspiracy controlling all the money in the world and using their secret power to persecute those good people not part of the tribe.

There are other sub-groups of anti-Semitism, but I believe that they will fall somewhere under these three categories. Interestingly, I don't see much evidence of significant theological anti-Semitism in the United States. The Christians, who traditionally viewed the Jews as a "damned people" due to their being the "murderers of God" (with regards to the crucifixion), do not seem to be of that mindset at the present time. And with regards to the Muslims in the U.S., I don't sense much of a passion to "kill the infidels," whether it be Jew or Christian, although this is certainly at the core of ISIS's and other radical Islamic groups' motivation for terrorism in the Middle East and Europe and those few domestic Islamic terrorist incidents that have taken place.

The Anti-Semitism Behind the Anti-Semitism

Before we proceed to discuss President Trump's role in this trend of increased anti-Semitism, let's note a longstanding Jewish perspective, which is that anti-Semitism is not really about Israeli policy, Jewish liberalism, or Jewish wealth and influence. Anti-Semitism is just a fundamental force in human history and is a part of the fabric of human society, due to the Jew's role in bringing moral behavior to humanity and representing that moral imperative, which grates on the instinctual desires that must be controlled to live a life that is just and merciful. The Talmud provides insights into the fundamental nature of anti-Semitism. The Talmud (Shabbos 89) cites the source of anti-Semitism using a play on words:

The Torah—the source of the Jewish system of laws, values and moral standards—was received at Mount Sinai. The Hebrew pronunciation of "Sinai" is almost identical to the Hebrew word for "hatred" —*sinah.* "Why was the Torah given on a mountain called Sinai?" asks the Talmud. "Because the great *sinah*—the tremendous hatred aimed at the Jew—emanates from Sinai." At Sinai Jews were told that there is one God, who makes moral demands on all of humanity. Consequently, at Sinai the Jewish nation became the target for the hatred of those whose strongest drive is to liberate mankind from the shackles of conscience and morality.
https://www.aish.com/sem/wtj/84684087.html

The implication here is that the Jew represents a morality that places powerful restraints on the instincts, and this creates frustration and anger among many of those who are not of the Jewish faith. This is, according to the Talmudic perspective, the fundamental cause for hatred of the Jews. Whether it is religious Jews who disdain the effectiveness of the Christian's "easy road to salvation" or liberal Jews who are imposing their own perspective of the moral high-ground, the psycho-dynamics are the same. To use classic Freudian terms, Jews, as a people, represent the superego (conscience) and anti-Semitism is the eternal battle of the id (instincts) with this superego. To stay with the Freudian analogy, usually the ego prevails (the reasoning, organizing element) and mediates between these two opponents. But sometimes the id rebels, overthrowing the ego, and acts without restraint to defeat the superego at all costs. According to this formulation, other factors such as economic conditions can awaken this conflict from dormancy, but the beast is always there and waiting for a propitious moment to pounce.

President Trump's Impact on Anti-Semitism

Whether President Trump is just an innocent bystander of the rise in American anti-Semitism, or is at least partially to blame for it, is impossible to know with any certainty. But we can identify those positions and views that he encourages and supports and those that he disdains. And being such a high-profile individual with a following of tens of millions of fans (and foes), as well as the subject of media that watches and reports his every word, it is reasonable to speculate that President Trump has a significant influence on societal trends, including anti-Semitism and Americans' current views about the Jews.

Trump's Support of Israel

Make no mistake that President Trump has been the greatest ally that the State of Israel has ever had in the American presidency. Whether that will change or not, I don't know. Whether Trump has any personal affinity or appreciation of Israel or whether this support is simply a tool to garner the Evangelical vote, I cannot say. But regardless of motivation, to this point, he has done what no U.S. president has ever done for Israel, including moving the U.S. Embassy to Jerusalem, recognizing Israel's sovereignty over the Golan Heights, and successfully isolating and debilitating Iran, Israel's greatest enemy. Even Israel's current plan to annex areas of the West Bank has met with no real opposition from the Trump administration.

But how has this bold Trumpian Zionism impacted anti-Semitism in the U.S.? It is a bit complex. For the Evangelicals and avid Trump fans it has probably increased their own positive perspective and support of Israel, even if it has not increased their love for the Jewish people as a whole. However, if one holds that the friend of my enemy is also my enemy, then Trump's alliance with Netanyahu and Israel has made Israel guilty by association for those who despise Donald Trump and all he stands for. Those who perceive Trump as an evil man and observe his close ties with Israel's Prime Minister Netanyahu, will tend to view Netanyahu as being evil as well, and feel justified in classifying Israel as an unjust, apartheid state. So, for those whose anti-Semitism is grounded in anti-Zionism, Trump has probably increased the level of hatred. What he loves, the left loathes.

Anti-Semitism and Trump's Support of Nationalism

Is President Donald Trump a white nationalist sympathizer? It seems incongruous or even unimaginable that someone who has so many familial connections and political alliances with Jewish people, and who is Israel's true champion in the world, could be aligned in any way with such an intensely anti-Semitic faction. Is there any substantial evidence to support this claim, often made by liberal media sources and the Democratic Party? It doesn't matter as much what Trump "really" thinks or feels. What matters is what the white nationalists *think* Trump thinks and feels. He does, in my opinion, embolden them by not categorically condemning them and occasionally making statements that appear to sympathize with "the white man's plight."

We saw some evidence of this in the recent mass killings carried out by those who self-identify as part of this group. The Australian-born suspect who shot and killed dozens of Muslim worshippers in Christchurch, New Zealand, published a manifesto praising Trump and Anders Breivik, the Norwegian white supremacist who murdered 77 people in Norway in 2011. The 74-page dossier hailed Trump as "a symbol of renewed white identity and common purpose."

Former Ku Klux Klan leader David Duke previously praised President Trump for tweeting about the "large scale killing of (white) farmers" in South Africa. Trump took to Twitter to announce that he had ordered Secretary of State Mike Pompeo to study South Africa land and farm seizures after Fox News host Tucker Carlson aired a segment on the topic. In my opinion, Trump is not a white supremacist or a racist, but he wants the votes of those who are. So, he leaves them wondering if maybe, he's really on their side but can't say so. Sadly, it's a lot of votes! It could be the margin between victory and defeat in 2020.

Trump's Opposition to Internationalism

President Trump is clearly unconcerned about the United States being viewed as a leader in standing up for the rights of the downtrodden or being at the forefront of international initiatives such as climate change legislation. He does not channel the famed statement on the Statue of Liberty, "Give Me Your Tired, Your Poor." This unsympathetic stance toward immigrants hoping to claim asylum due to their own countries' dangers and problems has endeared Trump to many Americans on the right who see immigration as a criminal and terrorist threat, as well as a cultural and economic one. Trump *does* want the U.S. to be respected for its strength, both economically and militarily. He has increased the military budget substantially. But beyond this, his international positions are guided purely by economic and military considerations for the betterment of the United States and its citizenry. This has helped Israel, as Trump and his cabinet view the Jewish State as a strategic ally and see little U.S. advantage to strengthening the Palestinians unless it will also assist Israel or some other ally in the region.

This diminishing of the U.S. government's concern for the "Palestinian plight," as compared to the Obama administration's, is mostly music to the ears of Jewish and Christian Zionists who have little love or sympathy for Palestinians. Trump's stance is, of course, vigorously opposed by the U.S. Muslim community and its representatives in Congress. Also, liberal Jewish American groups have protested, though not too intensely.

The impact of the COVID-19 pandemic on anti-Semitism in the United States may or may not be profound. If the economic contraction due to the virus is prolonged, one can reasonably speculate that the increased unemployment and poverty will increase anti-Semitism in America, as it has throughout history. Hopefully this challenging period will pass quickly and not awaken a dormant anti-Semitic strain that is certainly present within the new American nationalism. But if there is a true depression or even a prolonged recession, this could be a gamechanger. This catalyst, in combination with a growing nationalism, high unemployment, could result in a widespread perception of the Jews being as part of a monied, international cabal that is a danger to the United States and its people.

We will continue to explore whether the Trump presidency is related to the disturbing trend of growing anti-Semitism in the U.S. and whether it would be better or worse if a Democrat wins the White House in 2020.

Chapter 12
Donald and Jared—An American Pharaoh and His Joseph

The Biblical parallels are striking. President Trump often seems to be channeling the bombastic, larger-than-life characteristics of the biblical Pharaoh, and Jared Kushner is a modern-day version of Joseph, Pharaoh's trusted Jewish adviser. What are the similarities? Here are five that come to mind:

1-Both Trump and Pharaoh were faced with the mission of economic salvation for their respective "kingdoms." Pharaoh had to find a way to understand and respond to a potential economic catastrophe foretold in his troubling dreams of "7 fat cows followed by 7 lean cows." Trump too has based his presidency's success on a promise to revitalize a moribund American economy—thus his MAGA campaign slogan, "Make America Great Again."

2- Both Trump and Pharaoh have had limited faith in their professional cabinet appointments. Trump has set the presidential record for cabinet turnovers; Pharaoh dismissed the dream interpretations of his court magicians. Instead, both turned to Jewish *wunderkinds* to help solve their nations' most intractable problems. Pharaoh had his Joseph and Trump has his Jared Kushner.

3- Both Trump and Pharaoh had daughters that "fell for the Jewish people." Pharaoh had Batya, his daughter who rescued Moses from a basket in the river and raised him in the palace as her own. According to Jewish tradition, Batya later joined the Jewish people and left with them during the exodus from Egypt. Trump's daughter Ivanka converted to Judaism and is a practicing orthodox Jew married to Jared Kushner and raising Trump's Jewish grandchildren.

4-Both Trump and Pharaoh have provided the Jewish people with substantial support and sustenance. Pharaoh brought Joseph's family (who at that time were literally the entire "Children of Israel") down to Egypt to save them from the famine, providing them with a place in the country to live, prosper, and thrive. Trump is the greatest friend that the State of Israel (the contemporary "Children of Israel") has ever had in the presidency and has become its defender and protector on the world political stage.

5-Both Trump and Pharaoh are obsessed with building extremely large, grandiose structures that are primarily monuments to their personal greatness and prestige. Pharaoh had his royal palaces and pyramids; Trump has his Trump Palaces and Trump Towers and other properties that boldly proclaim the Trump name throughout the world, now and in the future (though I doubt they will last as long as the pyramids have). But the particular parallel that I would like to analyze here is the enormous level of power and influence that President Trump has given to his orthodox Jewish son-in-law, Jared Kushner, as his "senior adviser" in both domestic and foreign affairs of state—this despite Kushner's almost complete lack of expertise and experience in all of those areas for which he has been given broad authority. In the biblical story as well, Joseph, a 30-year-old Jewish man fresh from his prison cell and with no governmental experience, is elevated in a single day to the position of viceroy of Egypt and given absolute control over all of the country's economic decisions. Jared's rise was only slightly less spectacular and surprising than the biblical Joseph's in its speed and scope.

Who Is Jared Kushner?
How Did He Become Trump's "Right-Hand" Man?

Jared Kushner was born on January 10, 1981 (39 years old) and is the eldest son of real estate developer Charles Kushner. He was chief executive officer of the real estate holding and development corporation Kushner Companies, and of Observer Media, publisher of the *New York Observer*. He is the co-founder and part-owner of Cadre, an online real estate investment platform. Kushner was raised in a modern orthodox Jewish family and graduated from the Frisch School, a modern orthodox yeshiva high school in New Jersey. He graduated from Harvard in 2003 with a BA in government and from NYU with a dual JD/MBA degree. He has overseen a number of significant real estate development projects for the Kushner Companies. According to varied sources Jared Kushner's worth exceeds $500 million; some place it as high as $800 million.

Jared's Rapid Rise in the Trump Administration
More than any other person, except for the man himself, Jared Kushner was responsible for the election of Donald Trump as our 45th president. From the outset of the presidential campaign of his father-in-law, Kushner was the architect of Trump's digital,

online, and social media campaigns, enlisting talent from Silicon Valley to run a 100-person social media team dubbed "Project Alamo."

Kushner, together with Paul Manafort and Brad Parscale, hired Steve Bannon's firm Cambridge Analytica to support the Trump campaign. Kushner has also helped as a speechwriter, and was tasked with working to establish a plan for Trump's White House transition team. He was, for a time, seen as Trump's *de facto* campaign manager, succeeding Corey Lewandowski, who was fired in part on Kushner's recommendation in June 2016. He was intimately involved with campaign strategy, coordinating Trump's visit in late August to Mexico, and he is believed to be responsible for the choice of Mike Pence as Trump's running mate.

In my opinion, Trump attributes the astounding outcome of his election victory to Jared's unique intelligence, strategic cunning, and, perhaps to some extent, his "*mazel*" (good luck). For Trump, the world consists of "winners" and "losers." To Trump, Jared's pulling off the greatest election upset in American history makes him a "winner" of the highest caliber and he trusts that what Jared touches will be golden. Just as this seeming neophyte in political campaigning out-maneuvered and out-performed the best that Hillary Clinton's campaign megastructure of experts and billions of dollars could muster, Jared possesses a special magic, in Trump's mind, to accomplish incomparable results in other areas of governance. Trump also has complete confidence in Jared's loyalty due to the following attributes:

1-Jared being his son-in-law—he's not turning on the grandfather of his children, not to mention his father-in-law.
2-Jared did plenty of gray-area activities in the campaign that would assure that he would go down with the Trump ship if it ever were to sink.
3-Jared doesn't need the money from a book deal or a talk show.

Due to this combination of trust and confidence, Trump seemed to turn over much of the governance of the country to Jared early in his presidency. In March 2017 the thinkprogress.org web article "7 jobs Jared Kushner is now doing for the United States of America" provided the following list:

- Negotiating a Middle East peace deal
- Solving America's opioid epidemic
- Diplomacy with Mexico
- Diplomacy with China
- Reforming care for veterans
- Reforming the criminal justice system
- Reinventing the entire government and making it work like a business

https://thinkprogress.org/7-jobs-jared-kushner-is-now-doing-for-the-united-states-of-america-6f0a799462ed/

With a bit of presidential seasoning, Trump has distributed some of these responsibilities a bit more broadly, but Jared still stands high above all others in the cabinet with regards to his position and power. He has actually had some significant accomplishments These include:

1- Kushner's lead role on negotiations that culminated in the U.S.- Mexico-Canada Agreement was hailed by Senate Minority Leader Chuck Schumer (a staunch Trump opponent), rallied markets, handed Trump a major political victory, and earned Kushner the Order of the Aztec Eagle, Mexico's highest honor for foreigners.

2- Kushner helped to spearhead creation of the Formerly Incarcerated Reenter Society Transformed Safely Transitioning Every Person Act (FIRST STEP ACT, H.R. 5682) and its endorsement by the House Judiciary Committee on May 9, 2018, which is the first sweeping federal prison reform in decades.

3- He was involved in the sale of $100+ billion of arms to Saudi Arabia, and during a meeting with Saudi officials at the White House, negotiated costs with Lockheed Martin CEO Marilyn Hewson on a radar system to detect ballistic missiles.

The COVID-19 crisis has brought new responsibilities to Jared's already crammed portfolio. He has been charged by Trump to work with FEMA and the U.S. military to oversee getting essential medical and safety supplies to hospitals and other medical facilities. He is quoted in an April 4, 2020 National Public Radio article by Franco Ordonez ("Jared Kushner's Role In Coronavirus Response Draws Scrutiny, Criticism") regarding this role:

> As he recounted Thursday, the president had called him earlier that morning about reports he was hearing about critical shortages in the New York public hospital system. "I called Dr. [Mitchell] Katz, who runs the system, asked him which supply was the most supply he was nervous about," Kushner recalled. "He told me it was the N95 masks. I asked what his daily burn was, and I basically got that number, called up Adm. Polowczyk, made sure we had the inventory." Polowczyk is the director of fleet ordnance and supply at the U.S. Fleet Forces Command in Norfolk, Va.

Trump and Kushner—Charlatans? Geniuses? (Or Both)

I sometimes think that if Trump did everything he's done in the first two and a half years of his presidency—negotiated exactly the same deals, supported and pushed for the same policies, etc.—but had Obama write all of his speeches, his tweets, and everything else that came out of his mouth and fingers, Trump's approval would be 65% instead of 40% and he would be lauded as a great president. I could just see the headlines: "Perhaps the Greatest Out-of-the-Box Thinker of Modern Times!" or "The President Who Brought the Genius of Common-Sense to a Self-Absorbed Government Bloatocracy," etc. But as it is, Trump is truly loathed by half of America.

https://projects.fivethirtyeight.com/trump-approval-ratings/

For many on the left, there is nothing but disdain and disgust for him, based primarily on what he says (and tweets) and *how* he says (and tweets) it. Perhaps Trump knows that his bad behavior is the key to his success. I don't get a sense of Donald Trump being a "stable genius," but I am humbled in the face of his tremendous successes and would not be too quick to second-guess him. Jared's actual brilliance is also in question. He could turn out to be completely ineffective in his Middle East strategy; his grandiose plans may come to nothing. But at this point, he is also exceeding the expectations of his many detractors.

I, for one, will be following closely the developments of Jared's Middle East efforts, as well as his new gig as "Border Wall Czar" and "COVID-19 Supply Point Man". ." Will our American Pharaoh and his own personal Joseph actually be able to turn their bristling bravado and cunning, and hard-headed business-oriented negotiations, into a new path to peace for the Israelis and the Palestinians? Will Trump and Jared be able to get the fabled border wall built in time for the 2020 presidential elections? Will they be able to extract America from the clutches of the COVID-19 health/economic disaster? The whole world will be watching—half to see them succeed and the other half to gloat over their failures. Meanwhile the Trump/Kushner partnership continues at full steam, coronavirus or no coronavirus, and hopefully Kushner will be as good for Trump and America as Joseph was for Pharaoh and Egypt.

Chapter 13
The End of Jewish "Victimhood" in Trump's America

A diverse variety of groups consider themselves the victims of persecution and prejudice, or at the least, of being treated unfairly by other Americans, corporations, and governmental policies. Trump is seen by most of these groups as the "poster child" of this American injustice—especially by those viewing themselves and who are viewed by others as being victims of this mistreatment. Below is a partial list (in alphabetical order) of identity groups that are considered by themselves and by many of their fellow Americans to be the target of prejudice:

1-African Americans
2-Disabled people
3-Donald Trump! (according to him and his base)
4-Elderly people

5-Fetuses

6-Hispanic people

7-Illegal immigrants

8-Illegal immigrant children ("Dreamers")

9-Journalists

10-LGBTQ people

11-Muslim Americans

12-Obese people

13-People with mental illness

14-Poor people

15-Refugees from other countries seeking asylum

16-Small business owners

17-The planet Earth

18-White working-class people

19-Women

The much shorter list below consists of those American groups who are generally not considered to be victims of prejudice and injustice:

1-Affluent people

2-Asian Americans

3-Good-looking people

4-Highly educated people

5-Intelligent people

6-Jewish Americans (more about this later)

7-Middle-class white Christian Americans

8-Politicians (except Trump)

9-Straight people

10-Successful business people

11-Tall people

It is undoubtedly true that America is a place that has a long history of prejudice and discrimination, with hundreds of years of black slavery as its most despicable example of injustice to a particular group. In addition to slavery and legalized discrimination of the American black community for a century after the Civil War, our past includes the persecution of the Jews, Asians, Hispanics, Irish, Italians, Catholics, Muslims, and of course Native Americans. All have all been cruelly mistreated and excluded at various times of our history. But in spite of this checkered past and the long list of groups that view themselves, and are viewed by many others, as contemporary victims of prejudice, America is actually the place where, more than anywhere else on Earth, the dreams and aspirations of oppressed peoples have come true. That is *why* so many still want to immigrate to the U.S.

Many of those "huddled masses yearning to be free" who have come to its shores (or over its borders) in the past 250 years with no money, no connections, and little or no ability to speak English have emerged as successful, educated communities rising to the highest positions of power, wealth, and culture. In spite of America's long history of prejudice and injustice, the majority of the members of many immigrant groups have somehow managed to join the middle class, send their kids to college, own businesses, and enjoy the full spectrum of pleasures and opportunities the United States offers. Here is a partial list of immigrant groups that have experienced discrimination and yet have "made it" by just about any measure of success:

1-German Americans: The largest group of immigrants in the 1840-1870 period, it is now the largest ancestry group in the U.S. (44 million Americans claim German ancestry) with political, financial, and cultural success in all areas of American life.

2-Italian Americans: Though less than 25,000 were in the U.S. in 1870, four million immigrated between 1880 and 1914, 84% being from Southern Italy and Sicily. They have also achieved full power, influence, and general middle-class status.

3-Irish Americans: There are currently 33 million Americans who self-identify as Irish (compared to 6.6 million in Ireland!). There is a long history of immigration throughout the 19th and early 20th century with over three million immigrating between 1830 and 1890. Entering America in extreme poverty, religiously persecuted for their Catholic faith and economically excluded upon arrival, they are presently among the prominent, powerful, and affluent of America with full middle-class representation.

4-Eastern European Jews: Between 1880 and the onset of restrictive immigration quotas in 1924, over two million Jews from Russia, Austria-Hungary, and Romania came to America. The immigrants settled in the poorer neighborhoods of major cities. Living conditions in these neighborhoods were often cramped and squalid, and they found work in factories, especially in the garment industry. The children, grandchildren, and great-grandchildren of these immigrants became among the most successful people in the U.S., as measured by education, profession, affluence, and influence.

And more recently:

5-Chinese Americans: This group has had to overcome multiple discriminatory barriers in the U.S. including the "Chinese Exclusion Act" in 1882, which prohibited immigration from China for 10 years. By 1924 U.S. law prevented all Asians (except those from the U.S.-annexed Philippines) from obtaining citizenship or naturalization or from owning land. Since the 1940s there has been a steady, large immigration of Chinese Americans, and as of the 2016 census, there are more than five million in the U.S. They are now highly educated and earn a higher median income when compared to other American demographic groups. According to the 2010 U.S. Census, Chinese American men had a full-time median income of $57,061 and Chinese American women had a median income of $47,224. This was 30% higher than the national average.

6- Asian Indian Americans: According to the 2010 U.S. Census, the Asian Indian population in the United States grew from almost 1,678,765 in 2000 to 2,843,391 in 2010—a growth rate of 69.37%, one of the fastest-growing ethnic groups in the United States. Indian Americans continuously outpace every other ethnic group socioeconomically. According to a Pew Research study in 2015, of Indian Americans aged 25 and older, 32% had obtained a bachelor's degree and 40% had obtained a postgraduate degree, whereas of all Americans, 19% had obtained a bachelor's degree and 11% a postgraduate degree. The median household income for Indian immigrants in 2015 was much higher than that of the overall foreign- and native-born populations ($101,591 compared to $51,000 and $56,000 for overall immigrant and native-born households, respectively).
https://www.pewsocialtrends.org/fact-sheet/asian-americans-indians-in-the-u-s/

Anti-discrimination Laws and Policies in the U.S.

There is a widespread belief with regards to immigrant and other identity groups that they are discriminated against, and that American laws must be changed to address what many see as continued prejudice that exists in the system. But it should be noted that the United States has comprehensive governmental laws and corporate regulations in place to provide equal rights and accommodation to many of these groups who are viewed as victims of unfair treatment, outlawing discrimination against them.

The Civil Rights Act of 1964 prohibits unequal application of voter registration requirements, racial segregation in schools, employment, and public accommodations. The 1968 act expanded on previous acts and prohibited discrimination concerning the sale, rental, and financing of housing based on race, religion, national origin, and, since 1974, gender; since 1988, the act protects people with disabilities and families with children. Title VIII of the Civil Rights Act of 1968 is commonly referred to as the Fair Housing Act of 1968.

Sexual orientation and gender identity are not protected under the Fair Housing Act. Federal law in general does not protect gays and lesbians or other sexual minorities (transgender or transsexual) against discrimination in private housing. However, there are 22 states that have passed laws prohibiting discrimination in housing based on sexual orientation and gender identity. In the business and corporate world there is also a much less discriminatory culture than there has ever been before. In addition to adherence to the Civil Rights Act cited above, according to the Human Rights Campaign, 97% of Fortune 100 companies and 83% of Fortune 500 companies have non-discrimination policies that include gender identity as well.

The Success of LGBT Americans in the U.S.

The strongest expansions in LGBT rights in the U.S. have come from the Supreme Court. In four landmark rulings between the years 1996 and 2015, the Supreme Court invalidated a state law banning protected class recognition based upon homosexuality, struck down sodomy laws nationwide, struck down Section 3 of the Defense of Marriage Act, and made same-sex marriage a federal right. Twenty-two states plus Washington, D.C., and Puerto Rico outlaw discrimination based on sexual orientation, and 20 states plus Washington, D.C., and Puerto Rico outlaw discrimination based on gender identity or expression. Adoption of children by same-sex married couples is legal nationwide since June 2015 following the Supreme Court's decision in *Obergefell v. Hodges*.

Four years after marriage equality became the law of the land, Pete Buttigieg, an openly gay, married mayor from South Bend, Indiana, captured national attention in his campaign to become the Democratic Party nominee for the 2020 U.S. presidential election. He even won the Iowa Caucus and finished a close second in New Hampshire. On the campaign trail, he was often accompanied by his husband, Chasten. Voters on both sides of the political spectrum judged him on his policies rather than his sexual orientation.

Economically, the LGBT community has also made great strides. The National Gay & Lesbian Chamber of Commerce estimates a total U.S. LGBT population of between 16 million and 20 million people, and 1.4 million LGBT-owned businesses in the U.S. What's more, according to the U.S. Census Bureau and the Urban Institute, two-thirds of same-sex couples own their own home, and close to one-third of LGBT individuals have an annual income above $100,000.

Success, Victim Status, and the American Jewish Community
There is an inverse relationship between the success of a group and that group's status as a victim. Basically, the more successful a group is, the less they can claim victim status. To this end, the Jewish people have just about lost all victim "cred." They are too affluent, too powerful, and too successful to make a claim in this arena, in spite of historical, enduring, and recent spikes in anti-Semitism in the U.S. and abroad. Israel's emergence as an economic and military power, and the receding of the Holocaust

from cultural memory, has put the final "termination notice" on Jewish victimhood, and any protection this status afforded Jews. The gay community's success, as well as that of women, are significantly diminishing their victim status levels as well, and will continue to do so at a rapid pace. Asian Americans have become so successful in recent years that they are not even considered to be in the running for the "American Victim Prize."

Are Contemporary Americans Still Being Persecuted?

Of course, discrimination, unfairness, hatred, and prejudice exist in the United States. They always have and they always will. There will always be a number of situations where an individual or a group acts with prejudice and injustice against another. Good people still need to fight to continue to minimize it and address cases of it where individuals or groups are being treated unfairly. This struggle will continue.

But the relevant question for American governance is not whether prejudice continues to exist in America or not. What matters is whether the *level* of discrimination and prejudice are low enough, and the legal protections sufficient, to allow any group to succeed in a competitive field. Do people really have no prejudice or dislike for American Jews or Asian Americans? Of course, they do! But have the American Jewish or Asian Americans been prevented from succeeding economically or socially, as a group? I would have to answer, no. The same is true for LGBT people and many other American groups.

Also, it should be mentioned that, in spite of Trump's rhetorical bluster and fear-mongering, his presidency has not seen an increase in discriminatory laws or practices, when compared with Obama or Bush. In cases where he might attempt to exceed his authority on immigration or other human rights issues, the courts have successfully reined him in and maintained constitutional standards. The American court system has actually worked well, if not to everyone's full satisfaction, in protecting the basic rights of immigrants, Muslims, and other disempowered groups viewed as Trump targets.

There certainly were times in the past when discrimination did pose a high, almost impenetrable barrier, for many groups, Jewish people included. Barriers still exist and certain firms or residences may prefer one group over another. But the question is whether the level of this prejudice has been reduced to the point that members from all groups can and do succeed in America. This is all that can be expected of a country. It is similar to crime. People in the U.S. murder, rape, and steal. But America is, in general, a law-abiding society because the level of crime is low enough that it doesn't prevent most people from living their lives predominantly without being victims of criminal activity.

Crime will always be fought in order to further minimize it, but the country is still basically law-abiding. There could, theoretically, be such severe anti-crime laws that crime would be reduced to zero (think North Korea), but this would create new injustices and restrictions that would outweigh the benefits of the zero-crime rate.

Is "the System" to Blame?

This attempt to "blame it on the system" is something that all groups, including the Jewish people, indulge in. The difference in the economic, educational, and social success of some groups compared to others is complex. Whether it can be accurately attributed to institutionalized or personal prejudices being perpetrated against them is a difficult question. But there is much evidence from formerly persecuted, excluded groups now succeeding in the U.S. that runs counter to such a hypothesis. From the recent national uprising in the wake of the George Floyd killing, it is apparent that many Americans are firmly convinced that racism is still the main impediment to black and Hispanic success in contemporary America. Others do not agree that this is the case and are rebelling against some of the more extreme anti-racism positions of the left, which they perceive as irrational and fundamentally inaccurate. Trump has definitely tapped into this sentiment and will continue to do so as the left becomes more strident in identifying institutionalized prejudice as the cause of these inequalities, while the right continues to minimizes their impact. This division explains much of the appeal of Trump's outrageously politically incorrect manner of communicating with his supporters in which he aggressively belittles the left's cherished beliefs.

The Jewish Community: From Victim to Victimizer

It's a short path from being perceived as a victim to that of a victimizer. I fear that the Jewish community has, unfortunately, been traveling down that path, and this has greatly reduced their impact as a moral force. I am not accusing the Jewish people of actually *being* victimizers. But they are being perceived as such by a widening group of people. Wealth and power are being equated by the left with the status of victimizer. And as the Jewish people have moved to higher levels of affluence and influence in America, with many in high profile leadership position in technology, finance and media, they have, unwittingly taken on this victimizer status, in the minds of those particularly distrustful of wealth and power. Israel has also moved away from its former victim status, when it was a scrappy little country of Holocaust survivors surrounded and heavily outnumbers by Arabs who, outraged by the establishment of the Jewish state sought to finish Hitler's work and "drive the Jews into the sea". In just 70 years it has transformed itself into a militarily strong, wealthy country that wins wars, leads industries, and has an unapologetic, tough leader in Netanyahu, who is equated by many with President Trump in his attitudes and perspectives. The Palestinians are viewed by most of the world as victims of Jewish Israeli oppression. This impression has implications for how American Jews (whether they support Israeli policies or not) are viewed by their fellow Americans and the international community.

Regardless of the fact that Jewish people in the U.S. are still overwhelmingly liberal and supportive of the left, I don't think this will save them from the victimizer status that is really starting to stick. This issue showed itself blatantly in the Women's March in which there was a move to marginalize the Jewish groups due to their "victimizer" issues, with Women's March board member Linda Sarsour stating that feminists could not also be Zionists and that Zionists were Nazis. Sarsour, along with other Women's March board members Tamika D. Mallorry and Carmen Parez have also supported Louis Farrakhan whose anti-Semitic statements have compared Jews to termites.

I believe that even if the liberal and left Jewish communities "throw Israel under the bus," pledge their support for Palestine, and elect Ilhan Omar as "American Woman of the Year," while embracing all of the left's most extreme positions, it won't matter. In the minds of many on the left the following political algebra applies:

American Jews = Wealthy White Americans
Wealthy White Americans = Victimizers
Therefore: American Jews = Victimizer

Chapter 14

Understanding *Trumpspeak*
A Jewish Perspective

There has never been a person, let alone a politician, let alone a President of the United States, who uses language like Donald Trump. His choice of words, coining of phrases, timing, and verbal content may be a whole new phenomenon in the history of American life, or perhaps, even human civilization. But besides being a linguistic curiosity, what makes Trump's unique form of communication so fascinating is that, in spite of its almost unimaginable assault on the English language, it has made him the most successful politician in U.S. history.

No other person has ever risen from having absolutely no government or military experience to become the commander in chief and leader of the free world. And how did he accomplish this unprecedented feat? Not by his record of achievement or his good name, or through the endorsements of others (think former

Vice President Biden running on Obama's coattails). No. Donald J. Trump became president of this great nation because of one thing—what comes out of his mouth (and perhaps his tweets). Maybe he has benefited from our national obsession with celebrities, and he has received a bit of (unsolicited?) help from the Kremlin, as well as from the minds of his political gurus, Jared Kushner and Steve Bannon. But I think it is safe to say that the absolutely unique nature and power of *Trumpspeak* was the major factor in his unexpected relocation from the Trump Tower to Pennsylvania Avenue, and that this unique use of the English language was totally his own creation. But what is *Trumpspeak*?

The top choice on urbandictionary.com is:

A series of 2 or more sentences <u>devoid</u> of any real substance or <u>insight</u>, in which all <u>subsequent</u> sentences are just a rephrasing of the first. Actual examples given here include:
1-"I am very highly educated. I know words. I have the best words."
2-"I don't hate mexicans. I love mexicans. I employ thousands of mexicans and by the way mexicans love me. They respect me. Everyone loves me."

Comments by linguists that have analyzed *Trumpspeak* include the following:

1-It's basically the way people speak informally, being used in a formal context: Trump's language is much more "normal" than we might first think. He seems "unique" because he doesn't speak like a politician; "he speaks like everyone else." Jennifer Sclafani's two-year study of Trump's language concluded that although Trump "creates a spectacle" and "a brand" with his language, most of the features we associate with *Trumpspeak* ("a casual tone, a simple vocabulary and grammar, repetitions, hyperbole, and sudden switches of topic") are merely conventions of "everyday speech." She explains its apparent oddity: "It's just unusual to hear

it from a president speaking in a public, formal context."
https://www.youtube.com/watch?v=cpxCl8ylJgE

2- It confuses opponents and measures truth by what people believe: Lawrence Douglas of the *Guardian* explored some typical features of *Trumpspeak* and noted that Trump "overwhelmed his interviewer with such a profusion of misstatements, half-truths, dodges and red herrings that one grows dizzy trying to untangle it all." He analyzed *Trumpspeak*'s relationship with the truth, and drew the following conclusions:

- Truthful statements do not necessarily offer an accurate account of events in the world. They provide an approximation or exaggeration of something that might, in theory, have occurred.

- *Trumpspeak* confuses prophecy with honesty. If a news organization failed to correctly anticipate the president's win at the polls, *Trumpspeak* treats this as evidence of the falseness and mendacity of that organization's reportage about all of reality.

- Belief is a signal of truth. If his supporters believe him, then what Trump is saying must be true. *Trumpspeak* places no independent value on truth. The value of speech is to be measured, exclusively in terms of its effects. If a statement gets me closer to my goal, then it is valuable; if it does not, it is worthless.

  https://www.theguardian.com/commentisfree/2017/mar/24/donald-trumps-dizzying-time-magazine-interview-trumpspeak

3- It may be a sign of Trump having cognitive issues or cognitive decline. Sharon Begley's writing on Trump's language for STAT, provides an example of one of Trump's spontaneous utterances:

"…there is no collusion between certainly myself and my campaign, but I can always speak for myself—and the Russians, zero." When President Trump offered that response to a question at a press conference, it was another example of his tortured syntax, mid-thought changes of subject, and apparent trouble formulating complete sentences, let alone a coherent paragraph, in unscripted speech.

Begley's article notes how Trump "was not always so linguistically challenged." In interviews Trump gave in the 1980s and 1990s, he spoke articulately, used sophisticated vocabulary, inserted dependent clauses into his sentences without losing his train of thought, and strung together sentences into a polished paragraph. So, what's changed? It could be stress, or emotional upheaval. It could be strategic; "maybe Trump thinks his supporters like to hear him speak simply and with more passion than proper syntax." But Begley isn't convinced that it's just that. Research has shown that changes in speaking style can result from cognitive decline. For decades, studies have found that deterioration in the fluency, complexity, and vocabulary level of spontaneous speech can indicate slipping in brain function due to the effects of normal aging or due to some form of neurodegenerative disease. https://www.statnews.com/2017/05/23/donald-trump-speaking-style-interviews/

Some Other Defining Characteristics of *Trumpspeak*
I would like to add my own list here of definitive *Trumpspeak* characteristics not mentioned in the previous descriptions:

1- *Trumpspeak* projects confidence and fearlessness. Not only is Trump not afraid to go against the norms of politics as usual, he

2- is not afraid to go against all the norms of language! He won't be made to obey the silly "rules of grammar" or of syntax. His blustering blabber seems to proudly proclaim that "grammar is for nerds and weaklings."

3- *Trumpspeak* immunizes Trump from ever being considered a politician. Trump's manner of speaking exudes a sense of his being unguarded and unbound by conventions and the concerns that politicians (who almost everybody hates) have about how they "appear" to others. He actually speaks in the polar opposite way we expect a politician to speak. His speech brands him as the "anti-politician." If Trump spoke properly, one might suspect his being just another political hack.

4- *Trumpspeak* is grounded in attack, abuse, and degradation of his opponents. He almost never discusses an issue, *per se*. He will talk about it in terms of overcoming the insanity, stupidity, and unfairness of his opponents' views on that issue. He is always battling and attacking in some form. This also gives the impression of a strong, fearless person who is unafraid or even relishes conflict. Trump's language projects him as a "great warrior" even though he has never had any military experience. He may fight dirty, but he is a fighter, and if you believe he is fighting for you, this is a major plus.

5- *Trumpspeak* exudes independence. With the exception of formal speeches, no one else is writing most of what Trump says or tweets except him (no one could!). He is not controlled by other interests, or at least that's what his language portrays. This is why the "no collusion" conclusion is so important to Trump. If Trump was perceived as Putin's puppet, his status as "being his own man" would quickly deflate, and his supporters might abandon him.

Either/Ors About *Trumpspeak*
1-Is it spontaneous or contrived?
Is Trump really just speaking in an unguarded, spontaneous manner or are *Trumpspeak*'s distortions of language and syntax part of a premeditated plan to appeal to a particular portion of the electorate and/or confuse his opponents? My vote is that *Trumpspeak* is a natural and primarily spontaneous phenomenon.

2-Does Trump believe his own words or is it "flimflam"? Here I am not sure. On the one hand, Trump has held some version of his current nationalist views for decades. On the other hand, he does play freely with the truth and is not a stickler for accuracy. Some make the case that he is a habitual liar. There is at least some "flimflam" here, even if Trump basically believes in what he says.

3-Does *Trumpspeak* show Trump's intelligence or stupidity? If intelligence means a mastery of the details and the facts related to an issue, then *Trumpspeak* is a sign of Trump's ignorance. But if intelligence is a measure of one's clear sense of how to accomplish one's goals and ignore everything that doesn't contribute to this goal, then *Trumpspeak* is a sign of a unique intelligence.

4-Should *we* believe *Trumpspeak*? I would be very skeptical in believing what Trump says. He will use deception, exaggeration, and fear-mongering tactics to move his agenda forward. I am not saying whether Trump's objectives are the best ones for the country or not. What I am saying is that even if one supports Trump, I don't think it's prudent to take everything he says as the truth. Because it isn't!

5-Does *Trumpspeak* give you confidence in Trump or not? To some degree, confidence is contagious. Although many say that "deep down" Trump is an insecure person with a fragile ego, I do not agree. I think this is wishful thinking by many of his opponents. To me, *Trumpspeak*'s zany, aggressive boldness projects the president's 100% confidence in himself. This has resulted in many of his followers having great confidence in his leadership. In my experience, regardless of a person's competence or expertise, if that person is 100% confident in himself or herself and projects this state of mind effectively, a large percentage of people will be happy to choose this person as their leader.

Trumpspeak and Judaism's Perspective on Language

The Torah, Jewish law, and the ethical perspectives that have emerged from their indelible impact on the Jewish people give Jews a unique relationship to language and communication. There are three principles that define this Jewish perspective on language that would seem to put Jews at odds with _Trumpspeak_:

1-Speaking truthfully: There is a Jewish prohibition against _geneivas daas_ (literally, "theft of the mind") that prevents not only lying but also leaving a false impression. A simple example of _geneivas daas_ would be to invite someone to dinner merely to appear hospitable, knowing full well that the recipient would decline due to a prior commitment (a case discussed in the Talmud, _Chullin_ 94a). This prohibition against deception would seem to put the Jewish people at odds with Trump and almost all other politicians who habitually distort the truth in many clever and not so clever ways.

2-Perhaps even more reviled, from the Jewish perspective, than falsity in speech is the sin of insulting or embarrassing another. Statements throughout the Talmud and later Rabbinic sources emphasize how seriously the Rabbis took the prohibition of embarrassing others. Examples include:

> He who publicly shames his neighbor is as though he shed blood. (Talmud B.metzia 58b)

> Verbal wrong is more heinous than monetary wrong.

> Better it is for man to cohabit with a doubtful married woman rather than that he should publicly shame his neighbor. (Ibid, 59a) There was a poor person in the time of the Talmud and a fellow Jew, Mar Ukva, who would leave coins behind the poor man's door daily. One day the poor man wanted to find out who had been leaving coins for him. So, he waited until Mar Ukva and his wife stopped by and dropped off the coins. The pauper tried to follow them. When Mar Ukva noticed he was being followed he ran with his wife and hid in a hot furnace so as not to embarrass the man. (Talmud Ketuboth, 67b)

Rabbi Yonah in his famous work explains that the pain of shame is even worse than death itself (Gates of Repentance 3:129).

This perspective would also seem to put the Jewish people strongly at odds with Trump's penchant for publicly insulting and embarrassing others in an exceptionally aggressive manner.

3-Jewish practice includes a strict prohibition against *lashon hara* (evil talk)—this is a ban against speaking negatively about someone and spreading this information to others, even if it is true. The prohibition includes one who listens to this type of speech, as well. A person who regularly speaks *lashon hara* has no place in the World to Come (basically, a definition of a fundamentally evil person). The Talmud (Arakhin 15b) famously states that one who speaks *lashon hara* "kills" three people: the subject of the evil speech, the speaker, and the listener. The same page states that *lashon hara* is equal to the three cardinal sins: murder, idolatry, and adultery.

For the Jewish people, words matter, whether written or spoken. Language could be characterized as being sacred to the Jew. In the Jewish morning prayer service, we state that "God spoke and the world came into being." God spoke to Moses and the Jewish people at Mount Sinai, establishing the law and the nation. In Jewish tradition, the Torah is the written word of God and the Talmud is the oral communication of God. These are, for the religious Jew, the ultimate truths that must be guarded and passed down. There are endless references in Jewish texts to the issue of taking great care with regards to our words to make sure they are truthful and that they do not harm others.

So, what is the Jewish perspective on *Trumpspeak?* Among conservative, reform, unaffiliated, and secular Jews, with the exception of the Israelis, Trump is predictably spurned for his inaccurate way of speaking and his frequent insulting of others. This majority of the American Jews, who are predominantly liberal in their political views, attack *Trumpspeak* with great intensity.

One of the most dramatic cases of this perspective occurred at the Tree of Life Synagogue in Pittsburgh, where 11 Jewish congregants were killed in October 2018 by an anti-immigrant terrorist. The synagogue members made it clear that they did not want President Trump to pay them a visit. A former president of the synagogue in Pittsburgh said Donald Trump would not be welcome in the city and labeled the president a "purveyor of hate speech." The comments followed an open letter signed by a coalition of local Jewish leaders and published by the Pittsburgh chapter of Bend The Arc, a progressive advocacy group, that also called for the president to avoid the city.

But among American Orthodox Jews and those who are strongly Zionistic in their views, Trump is, for the most part, given a pass. The National Council of Young Israel condemned the Jewish people of Pittsburgh and elsewhere who protested Trump. "We are saddened that some even within our Jewish community have attacked The President and his policies instead of using this period as one of healing. This is not a time for political attacks." The Young Israel organization heaped praise on President Trump, saying, "It is important that certain facts are made clear about President Trump that unfortunately are not verbalized often enough by the American Jewish community. President Trump is the best friend Israel has had in the White House."
https://bigleaguepolitics.com/orthodox-rabbi-organization-national-council-of-young-israel-praises- president-trump/

What is it about Trump that allows for this tolerance of *Trumpspeak*'s dishonesty and insulting nature by many orthodox Jews and Zionists? I see three possibilities:

1-Simple self-interest: Perhaps it is as simple as Trump delivering on issues important to those Jewish groups that support him. Even though his Jewish supporters may abhor his language choice, his lack of truthfulness, and profound insensitivity to the feelings of others, they support him because he helps them achieve their objectives. But I don't think this fully explains his fervent support among the orthodox and Zionists.

2-Low expectations from politicians and people who are not Jewish: Perhaps the orthodox Jews do not expect stellar behavior from those outside the fold, and since Trump is not a Jew, he can't be expected to conduct himself in a proper manner. But still, he supports Israel and many other issues of value to the Jewish people. So, for better or worse, he is our man. But I still don't think this perspective gets to the heart of his support among the Jewish and orthodox communities.

3-A sense that his essential statements are true and that his attacks are against evil people and views that must be defeated, even if one has to fight dirty. This is the one I think explains the phenomenon of Jewish support best. Those Jews who are true supporters of Trump believe that he is a basically decent person with flaws, who is fighting a noble fight against the liberal insanity that equates terrorism with Zionism, believes gender is a choice, embraces dangerous socialist positions, and threatens the damage and destruction of America and Israel. It is a fact that Trump is insulting and distorts the truth. But in the view of his fervent supporters he does this to accomplish a noble and higher purpose—to battle evil. This makes it not only permissible; it makes it the right thing to do! Of course, the more liberal Jews, who are part of the group that Trump attacks as possessing this distorted, evil nature, would not concur with this perspective!

In his ethical work, "Strive for Truth," Rabbi Eliyahu Dessler, a popular orthodox British rabbinic scholar from the early twentieth century, explains that truth should not be defined based on what is factually true, but what is in conformity with the will of God; i.e., the Torah—whereas falsehood is not necessarily something that is factually false, but rather that which is contrary to the values of the Torah. Thus, even if a certain statement may appear false factually, if making it furthers an important Torah value, then, in fact, one has "adhered to the truth."

This seems to me to be a slippery slope. But I believe that those American and Israeli Jews, religious or not, who believe in Trump believe that his lies are a form of truth because they move us toward the good and away from perceived evil. His attacks are attacks against evil people and destructive ideas, which is also a noble action and one in which Judaism allows the deception and insulting of the enemy. This perspective may not be true of all Jews who vote for Trump, but for his true fans among the Jewish people, I think this explanation is a pretty good fit.

Chapter 15

When Donald Met Bernie:
The New Socialist Chic and the American Jewish Community

A September 2018 poll found that 31% of American millennials (defined by this poll as those born between 1982 and 2004) identify as being either a democratic socialist or a socialist. The same poll also found that 48% of Democratic millennials self-identify as either democratic socialist or as socialists. https://info.marublue.net/acton/attachment/36213/f-0012/1/-/-/-/-/BuzzFeed%20News.pdf

Other surveys have found an even larger percentage of millennials rejecting capitalism. In "A Majority of Millennials Now Reject Capitalism, Poll Shows," reporting on a Harvard University survey of young adults from age 18 to 29 found 51 percent not supporting capitalism (*Washington Post*, April 26, 2016). The article "Most Young Americans Prefer Socialism to Capitalism, New Report Finds" noted that 51 percent of young people are positive about socialism, compared with only 45 percent who view capitalism favorably (CNBC, August 14, 2018). The article "Millennials Would Rather Live in Socialist or Communist Nations than Under Capitalism" stated that only 42 percent of millennials prefer capitalism to socialism or communism (*Washington Times*, November 4, 2017).

What about the Jewish millennials' view of socialism? The previously cited Democratic millennial statistic of 48% identifying as socialists is most relevant to the U.S. Jewish population, since according to a 2018 Pew Research report, 79% of American Jews voted Democratic in the most recent midterm elections. I don't think that millennial Jews would be *less* Democratic in affiliation than the general Jewish population. Usually the younger members of a group tend toward the political left of the group average. So, it seems reasonable to assume that a majority of Jewish millennials would identify as democratic socialists or socialists. But before we dive into the Jewish community participation in the current political shift, it is important to define our terms.

There are two designations that are often used to describe those embracing socialistic leaning policies: 1-social democrat and 2-democratic socialist. Are these similar-sounding terms describing the same political philosophy? Practically, they are often used interchangeably by most people and many journalists. There seems to be confusion, even among those claiming etymological and political expertise, regarding their meanings. The website democraticunderground.com defines these two political positions as being quite distinct from one another:

In its posting "'Social Democracy' vs. 'Democratic Socialism'" it states:

> Social democracy is a political ideology that supports economic and social interventions to promote social justice within the framework of a capitalist economy, and a policy regime involving welfare state provisions, collective bargaining arrangements, regulation of the economy in the general interest, redistribution

of income and wealth, and a commitment to representative democracy. Social democracy thus aims to create the conditions for capitalism to lead to greater egalitarian, democratic and solidaristic outcomes; and is often associated with the set of socioeconomic policies that became prominent in Western and Northern Europe—particularly the Nordic model in the Nordic countries—during the latter half of the 20th century.

Democratic Socialism is a political ideology advocating a democratic political system alongside a socialist economic system, involving a combination of political democracy with social ownership of the means of production. Although sometimes used synonymously with "socialism," the adjective "democratic" is often added to distinguish itself from the Marxist–Leninist brand of socialism, which is widely viewed as being non-democratic (i.e., brought about through revolution, not by being voted in-RB). Ultimately democratic socialists believe that reforms aimed at addressing the economic contradictions of capitalism will only cause more problems to emerge elsewhere in the economy, so that capitalism can never be sufficiently "humanized" and must ultimately be replaced by socialism.
https://www.democraticunderground.com/12511042313

So, according to definitions of democraticunderground.com we do have a fundamental difference between these political positions. Social democracy is a form of capitalism (private ownership, free markets) but with heavy regulation of industry and government ownership/control of key services, such as utilities, transportation, education, and healthcare. This is, to some degree, what we already have in the United States. Democratic socialism, on the other hand, is a voter-driven move of the government toward true socialism, in a process by which the capitalist system is replaced by one where state ownership dominates the economy (think of the former Soviet Union with the leadership being voted into power instead of taking over by violent revolution).

But other experts, such as Meriam-Webster.com, cite no meaningful distinction between democratic socialism and social democracy, using these two terms interchangeably to express a form of more highly regulated capitalism, with both being distinguished from any type of actual socialism—even one brought about by democratic means (i.e., being voted in). Merriam-Webster explains:

> In the modern era, "pure" socialism has been seen only rarely and usually briefly in a few Communist regimes. Far more common are systems of <u>social democracy</u>, now often referred to as democratic socialism, in which extensive state regulation, with limited state ownership, has been employed by democratically elected governments (as in Sweden and Denmark) in the belief that it produces a fair distribution of income without impairing economic growth.
> <u>https://www.merriamwebster.com/dictionary/social%20demo</u>
> <u>cracy</u>

Is the American left's embrace of social democracy (aka democratic socialism) really a shunning of capitalism in favor of a state-owned and controlled economy? And what about Bernie Sanders, the veritable "Pied Piper" of this transformation of social democracy from an extreme fringe position to the middle of the U.S. political mainstream? Is he in favor of true socialism, to be achieved through voter decisions, or is he just envisioning an incrementally more regulated capitalism with a cool, radical name? Does Bernie really want to turn Apple, Microsoft, Citibank, and Chase into government-owned enterprises, or is he just trying to make "kinder, gentler" billionaires and moderate what he views as gross excesses of the current capitalist system?

How Red Is Bernie?

As the vanguard and granddad of the recent mainstreaming of socialist-leaning policies, it's instructive to delve into Senator Sanders' views and political history. Let's dig in a bit and see what we find. After all, he has been on the scene for a *long* time and his history is more or less public record. It is certainly true that he has had some serious flirtations with countries and leaders that are true socialists. A 2015 article in the *National Review* cites some of these "Commie" dalliances. For example:

During Bernie's Burlington, Vermont, mayoral tenure in the 1980s, he formed an alliance with the Soviet city of Yaroslavl, 160 miles northeast of Moscow. When in 1988 he married his wife, Jane, the 46-year-old mayor decided that the Soviet Union would be a perfect place for his honeymoon. During the trip, which included Red Square in Moscow, Leningrad (the Soviet name for St. Petersburg), and the rundown Volga city of Yaroslavl, he noted the much lower level and quality of Soviet services, but also was highly critical of the cost of housing and healthcare in America while praising the Soviet Union for their lower prices. He visited Cuba and tried to meet Fidel Castro, which didn't work out. So, he had to settle for a meeting with Havana's mayor instead. He returned home calling the Cuban revolution "far deeper and more profound than I had understood it to be."

Back in 1985 he attended the celebrations held to mark the sixth anniversary of the Sandinista Marxist revolution in Nicaragua and denounced the activities of the Reagan administration, which he said was under the influence of large corporations:

> "In the long run, I am certain that you will win," Sanders wrote, "and that your heroic revolution against the Somoza dictatorship will be maintained and strengthened."
> https://www.nationalreview.com/corner/bernie-sanderss-soviet-honeymoon- john-fund/

Regardless of these photo-ops and genuflections to actual revolutionary communist/socialist regimes, Bernie, at his current stage of political development, is not publicly avowing true-red socialist positions or rhetoric. Paul R. Gregory of the *Hoover Institution Journal* of Stanford University wrote in May of this year:

> The largest American socialist party, the Democratic Socialists of America (DSA), unlike Sanders, openly declares its intent to abolish capitalism as we know it. A staff writer for a DSA house publication could not be clearer: "In the long run, democratic socialists want to end capitalism…we want to end our society's subservience to the market." Does Sanders agree? That is the question…. The Democratic Socialists of America has grown from 6,000 to 60,000 dues-paying members in the last eight years and counts two members of Congress—with Alexandria Ocasio-Cortez (AOC) and Rashida Tlaib in its ranks.
> https://www.hoover.org/research/how-socialist-bernie-sanders

Bernie Sanders, interestingly, according to this article, is *not* a DSA party member. This distancing of himself from the actual American socialists, along with Bernie's other policy positions, are seen by many as clear evidence that he simply wants to extend the American welfare system launched by FDR when he started Social Security (1935) and which was extended in LBJ's "Great Society" programs of Medicaid (1965) and Medicare (1966). Bernie is viewed by his more moderate supporters as wanting to logically extend this well-established welfare system (some prefer the term "safety net") to areas such as healthcare and education. This expansion, they explain, is now required due to the tremendous increase in the cost of healthcare as it has dramatically expanded technologically and pharmacologically, as well as the prohibitive cost of higher education. Also, higher education has morphed from an institution for the upper class and exceptionally talented to become a basic requirement by all who seek to successfully compete for meaningful and well-compensated jobs. FDR is one of Bernie's heroes. Sanders stated in a campaign speech:

> Over eighty years ago, Franklin Delano Roosevelt helped create a government that made transformative progress in protecting the needs of working families. Today, in the second decade of the twenty-first century, we must take up the unfinished business of the New Deal and carry it to completion.
> https://www.jacobinmag.com/2019/06/bernie-sanders-speech-democratic-socialism- new-deal-fdr

True, Sanders is also a longtime fan of Eugene Victor Debs (November 5, 1855-October 20, 1926) who was an American socialist, political activist, trade unionist, one of the founding members of the Industrial Workers of the World (IWW), and five times the candidate of the Socialist Party of America for president of the United States. Supposedly, Sanders still has a portrait of Debs hanging on the wall of his Senate office.

As of this writing, Bernie's chances of becoming President Sanders have faded. He has suspended his campaign and it seems that Joe Biden will be the Democratic nominee. But whether Sanders becomes America's commander in chief or not, his campaigning and influence have brought the dream of an American Scandinavian-styled social democracy into the hearts and minds of millions of Americans. This vision has showed up in the positions Elizabeth Warren, Kamala Harris, Cory Booker, and others who, along with Sanders, have vied for a chance at the Oval Office chair. Even Joe Biden, "Mister Moderate," is talking about "Medicare for All," though he doesn't want to eliminate the private health insurance sector (yet). We live in a time when labels that once were considered radical have quickly shifted to becoming not only accepted, but chic, and what some consider superior and more enlightened than what was previously considered normal and proper. It will be instructive to see what socialist-inspired policies make it into the 2020 official Democratic platform, as well as how the economic contraction due to COVID-19, with its extremely high level of job loss and bankruptcies, impacts the comfort level of socialism in the U.S.

The Socialist Chic
- Partnering is chic; marrying is not.
- Gay marriage is chic; straight marriage is not.
- Being a socialist is chic; being a capitalist is not.

Since socialism is chic, many young liberal-left Jewish people want to be socialists! For some, it is as simple as that. And, by the way, this is certainly not the Jewish socialists' first rodeo. Bernie is an old-time New York Jewish socialist from Brooklyn. And the Jewish connection to socialism in Europe, America, and Israel is quite significant and longstanding. The current situation of many Jews, young and old, embracing socialist ideas is not a new romance as much as the rekindling of an old flame.

Jews, Socialism, and the Roots of the American Left
You might say that Jews were the first people that inculcated socialist ideals into a system of governance. Where does it first show up? In the Torah! According to Torah dictates, the land of Israel, once conquered, was divided up into 12 sections with each Jewish tribe receiving its portion. These sections were then divided among the families of each of the 12 tribes. At that point, families could buy and sell land and expand (or reduce) their stake by purchase or sale. But, after 50 years, on what was termed "the Jubilee," all land of Israel would return to its original distribution with the tribes and families having just what they had at the beginning. This cycle would take place every 50 years. This is certainly a form of socialist-style wealth redistribution. But let's jump to much more modern times to explore the Jewish community's involvement in socialist activities and governance.

Jewish socialism flourished in 1880s America with mass Jewish immigration from Eastern Europe. Among those who immigrated from Russia were some of those Jews who had been active in the early Russian revolutionary movement. Some aligned themselves with anarchists or Marxist socialists. The Workmen's Circle fraternal order and aid society, and the Yiddish newspaper *The Jewish Daily Forward* (today just *Forward*), became popular institutions in the Lower East Side Jewish community. Jewish socialists controlled many of the Jewish trade unions, especially in the garment industry. In 1914, the Lower East Side sent socialist labor lawyer Meyer London to Congress with a pledge to represent both working-class and immigrant Jewish interests. As most people know, socialist Zionists were at the heart of the early Zionist movement, and sought to combine Zionism with socialist principles. There was much conflict and disagreement among socialist Jews as to whether a Jewish state (with its specifically Jewish focus) could be said to embrace the true internationalism that was at the core of Marxist ideology. Still, many socialist elements did take root in the State of Israel, expressed most purely in the Israeli kibbutz movement.

Why Now?

Socialism usually rises in popularity during times of economic hardship. So why, when the United States economy was thriving and unemployment was so low, was there a seeming resurgence of this long moribund political modality? Jewish Americans seemed, before the coronavirus pandemic, to be doing quite well, economically. So why the attraction? Let's list a few of the most likely causes:

1- "Heroes have arisen." For those who propound the "Great Men" (or "Great Women") theory of history, people are attracted to exceptional individuals, and this is the catalyst for the popularity among the masses for the ideas these charismatic "heroes" propound. Although Bernie and AOC are not exactly Napoleons, they are personalities that seem to connect with millions of people, and have energized the socialist debate. But as the saying goes, "There is nothing as powerful as an idea whose time has come." So, I think that we can assume that there is something besides these media-savvy socialists—something about the current times in America—that is responsible for socialism's current rise.

2-President Donald Trump. For many, Trump has damaged the "brand" of capitalism and many are looking for cover in calling themselves anything else. Trump is viewed by the liberal left, Jews included, as simply vile—a cruel, selfish, egotistical, shallow, bully who loves money, power, and prestige, with little interest in justice, mercy, or responding to the larger issues that confront mankind. Whether this is true or not is not the issue. But undoubtedly, many on the left believe it is and do not want to be on his team.

3-Income disparity. Technology has facilitated the expansion of businesses to international markets, which themselves have increased in wealth and buying power. This situation has resulted in a phenomenal growth in the value of these companies, and those who own and run them or have the disposable income to invest in them (stock market). But it has not increased the salaries or worth of those who do not. This has resulted in an unprecedented income disparity between the top and everybody else. Seeing those with excess billions they don't know what to do with, and comparing them with one's own struggle to pay student loans, mortgages, college costs, rising housing and food costs, etc., is making formally capitalist-minded people ready to embrace a more aggressive form of wealth redistribution.

4-Capitalism has become unbearably invasive. With data mining, the 24/7 advertising and promoting of products and services, people are seeking relief. Marketing seeps into every moment of our day and some are getting a bit disgusted with the endless deceptions, persuasions, and manipulations that are associated with it all. This major societal change is also the direct result of technological growth, symbolized by the smartphone, and has put capitalism in a highly negative light for many who are completely dependent on this technological "Matrix

5-Scandanavia!!! The land of beautiful, tall, blonde people who have a lifetime safety net from birth to death and are rated as among the world's happiest humans! No vicious Bolsheviks here! Maybe, the socialist democrats wonder, America can graft a bit of these desirable traits onto its own national DNA. There is a large dose of wishful thinking here due to the size and heterogenicity of the American population compared to that of the Scandinavian countries, as well as our high rates of federal debt and poverty rates.

But have no fear. Americans, even on the left and far left, do not really want to give up the freedom and opportunities that only capitalism can bestow. For the most part, the social democrats just want to tweak capitalism enough with kinder and gentler adjustments to give it a better brand, lower their economic stress levels, and distance themselves from the perceived ugly American in the White House. It is true that America will soon be a greener, energy-efficient country, and that the very rich will be more highly taxed. This will happen whether Trump gets elected or not. It's just a matter of the pace of this change. But this being said, money, luxurious living, and power will still have their allure and those that desire them will work very hard to obtain them.

Privilege and opulence will endure in America. It's just that wealth will have a few more green, gentle-looking fig leaves to give it cover and keep the middle class and poor people content enough to stay busy at their labors, so that they can spend their money and keep the capitalist engine running.

Chapter 16

Democratic De-Zionation and Trump's Israeli Romance

"De-Zionation" is a word I am coining to mean the transformation of an individual or group from being a supporter of Israel to being a detractor of the Jewish State. The question is whether the Democratic Party leadership, party members, or both are undergoing a process of De-Zionation at the present time. A watershed moment in determining whether this De-Zionation is taking place will be the party's position on Israel in its official Democratic platform statement for the upcoming 2020 presidential election. I would like to compare the three most recent Democratic platforms' official statements on Middle East policy.

In 2008 the Democratic platform's Middle East section stated:

> For more than three decades, Israelis, Palestinians, Arab leaders, and the rest of the world have looked to America to lead the effort to build the road to a secure and lasting peace. Our starting

point must always be our special relationship with Israel, grounded in shared interests and shared values, and a clear, strong, fundamental commitment to the security of Israel, our strongest ally in the region and its only established democracy. That commitment, which requires us to ensure that Israel retains a qualitative edge for its national security and its right to self-defense, is all the more important as we contend with growing threats in the region—a strengthened Iran, a chaotic Iraq, the resurgence of Al Qaeda, the reinvigoration of Hamas and Hezbollah. We support the implementation of the memorandum of understanding that pledges $30 billion in assistance to Israel over the next decade to enhance and ensure its security.

It is in the best interests of all parties, including the United States, that we take an active role to help secure a lasting settlement of the Israeli-Palestinian conflict with a democratic, viable Palestinian state dedicated to living in peace and security side by side with the Jewish State of Israel. To do so, we must help Israel identify and strengthen those partners who are truly committed to peace, while isolating those who seek conflict and instability, and stand with Israel against those who seek its destruction. The United States and its Quartet partners should continue to isolate Hamas until it renounces terrorism, recognizes Israel's right to exist, and abides by past agreements. Sustained American leadership for peace and security will require patient efforts and the personal commitment of the President of the United States. The creation of a Palestinian state through final status negotiations, together with an international compensation mechanism, should resolve the issue of Palestinian refugees by allowing them to settle there, rather than in Israel. All understand that it is unrealistic to expect the outcome of final status negotiations to be a full and complete return to the armistice lines of 1949. Jerusalem is and will remain the capital of Israel. The parties have agreed that Jerusalem is a matter for final status negotiations. It should remain an undivided city accessible to people of all faiths.

In 2012 the platform's Middle East section stated:

President Obama and the Democratic Party maintain an unshakable commitment to Israel's security. A strong and secure Israel is vital to the United States not simply because we share strategic interests, but also because we share common values. For this reason, despite budgetary constraints, the President has worked with Congress to increase security assistance to Israel every single year since taking office, providing nearly $10 billion in the past three years. The administration has also worked to ensure Israel's qualitative military edge in the region. And we have deepened defense cooperation-including funding the Iron Dome system-to help Israel address its most pressing threats, including the growing danger posed by rockets and missiles emanating from the Gaza Strip, Lebanon, Syria, and Iran. The President's consistent support for Israel's right to defend itself and his steadfast opposition to any attempt to delegitimize Israel on the world stage are further evidence of our enduring commitment to Israel's security.

It is precisely because of this commitment that President Obama and the Democratic Party seek peace between Israelis and Palestinians. A just and lasting Israeli-Palestinian accord, producing two states for two peoples, would contribute to regional stability and help sustain Israel's identity as a Jewish and democratic state. At the same time, the President has made clear that there will be no lasting peace unless Israel's security concerns are met. President Obama will continue to press Arab states to reach out to Israel. We will continue to support Israel's peace treaties with Egypt and Jordan, which have been pillars of peace and stability in the region for many years. And even as the President and the Democratic Party continue to encourage all parties to be resolute in the pursuit of peace, we will insist that any Palestinian partner must recognize Israel's right to exist, reject violence, and adhere to existing agreements…. Jerusalem is and will remain the capital of Israel. The parties have agreed that Jerusalem is a matter for final status negotiations. It should remain an undivided city accessible to people of all faiths.

The 2012 platform was quite similar to the 2008 platform statement except that it did not make it explicit that Palestinian refugees would settle only in the proposed Palestinian state and not in Israel, as the 2008 platform statement does. Instead it states that the "two states for two people would contribute to regional stability and help sustain Israel identify as a Jewish and democratic state." There is a bit more room here for a Palestinian population refugee incursion into Israel, which is more categorically excluded in 2008's language, which states, "The creation of a Palestinian state through final status negotiations, together with an international compensation mechanism, should resolve the issue of Palestinian refugees by allowing them to settle there, *rather than in Israel.*"

There was also significant drama in 2012 regarding the retaining of the statement "Jerusalem will remain the capital of Israel," which was first included and then removed, until President Obama had it reinserted. In addition, the 2012 platform no longer stated, "All understand that it is unrealistic to expect the outcome of final status negotiations to be a full and complete return to the armistice lines of 1949," as was stated in the 2008 platform. In 2016 the platform's Middle East section stated:

> A strong and secure Israel is vital to the United States because we share overarching strategic interests and the common values of democracy, equality, tolerance, and pluralism. That is why we will always support Israel's right to defend itself, including by retaining its qualitative military edge, and oppose any effort to delegitimize Israel, including at the United Nations or through the Boycott, Divestment, and Sanctions Movement. We will continue to work toward a two-state solution of the Israeli-Palestinian conflict negotiated directly by the parties that guarantees Israel's future as a secure and democratic Jewish state with recognized borders and provides the Palestinians with independence, sovereignty, and dignity. While Jerusalem is a matter for final status negotiations, it should remain the capital of Israel, an undivided city accessible to people of all faiths. Israelis deserve security, recognition, and a normal life free from terror and incitement. Palestinians should be free to govern themselves in their own viable state, in peace and dignity.

The 2016 platform statement supports a two-state solution but does not address the Palestinian refugee issue at all and limits the commitment to Israel to its being a "secure and democratic Jewish state with recognized borders." The change in wording with regards to Jerusalem is also noteworthy. While in 2012 the platform stated, "Jerusalem *is and will* remain the capital of Israel," in 2016 it stated, "While Jerusalem is a matter for final status negotiations it *should* remain the capital of Israel." Some significant slippage here. Even so, this 2016 platform language was not at all to the liking of a number of delegates who sought a much stronger Pro-Palestinian, anti-Israel position. The Associated Press reported at the time that the final discussion about the platform "centered on the Israel-Palestinian conflict":

> The committee defeated an amendment by (Bernie) Sanders supporter James Zogby that would have called for providing Palestinians with 'an end to occupation and illegal settlements' and urged an international effort to rebuild Gaza," measures which Zogby said Sanders helped craft. Instead, AP reports, the adopted draft "advocates working toward a 'two-state solution of the Israel-Palestinian conflict' that guarantees Israel's security with recognized borders 'and provides the Palestinians with independence, sovereignty, and dignity." Citing these "moral failures" of the platform draft, (Cornell) West abstained during the final vote to send the document to review by the full Platform Committee next month in Orlando, Florida. "If we can't say a word about TPP (Trans-Pacific Partnership), if we can't talk about Medicare-for-All explicitly, if the greatest prophetic voice dealing with pending ecologically catastrophe can hardly win a vote, and if we can't even acknowledge occupation...it seems there is no way in good conscience I can say, 'Take it to the next stage,'" West declared before the assembly.
> https://www.timesofisrael.com/democrats-approve-platform-with-sanders-mark-but-not-on-israel/

As almost all of the issues Cornell West mentioned in his rejection of the 2016 platform statement moved from the fringe to the mainstream of the 2020 Democratic Party presidential candidates' positions, it will be most intriguing to see what the final language of the 2020 Democratic platform will be, and whether there will be a noticeable erosion in the support for Israel as a Jewish state with Jerusalem as its capital. Will the term "occupation" be included? Will there be any language openly supporting the Palestinian "struggle"? We will have to wait and see.

Meanwhile, let's take a look at some of the dramatic and unprecedented events that have occurred during Trump's tenure that bespeak of this Democratic "De-Zionation" phenomenon. While we are at it, we can try to illuminate the nature and motivation of President Trump's continuing romance with the State of Israel and Prime Minister Netanyahu, and explore how this relationship is turning the stomachs of staunch anti-Trumpers that compose a majority of the Democratic Party officials and membership, and how this political dyspepsia is impacting Democrats' views of the Jewish State.

The Witch's Brew of De-Zionation

There is a witch's brew of five poisonous ingredients that have recently combined to concoct a deadly potion that, when swallowed, transforms a Democratic Zionist into a Democratic Israel-basher. Here is the De-Zionation potion's formula:

1-First, add a drop of American Ambassador to Israel David Friedman's unnuanced support of Netanyahu and Israeli nationalists' goals, including recognition of the Golan Heights as part of Israel and of annexing West Bank territories, while placing a Palestinian state on the back burner or completely off the stove.

2-Add Trump's moving of the American Embassy to Jerusalem over the protests of the Palestinians and many on the left in the Jewish community.

3-Mix in four drops of young, media-savvy, influential Democratic congresswomen of color ("The Squad") who have included among their core principles strident support of the Palestinian "struggle," as well as the demonizing of the Israeli government under Netanyahu (who they view as, basically, a Trump clone).

4-Now pour in a full cup of middle western and southern liberal loathin', gun-totin', "abortion-is-murder" toutin' fundamentalist

Christian Republicans who have made unbridled support of Israel one of the most passionate litmus test positions of their faith.

5-Sprinkle about 500 Trump tweets about loving Israel, Netanyahu, and Jerusalem and disparaging Palestinians.

6-Have CNN, MNBC, the *New York Times*, and the *Washington Post* stir the potion pot thoroughly and continuously.

And—voila! No liberal/left Jewish Democrat stands a chance against the overwhelming power of this elixir once he or she has swallowed it! It doesn't even taste too bad!

Zionism has now managed to become inextricably enmeshed with everything that turns the stomachs of any self-respecting liberal Democrat. Meanwhile, the Palestinian "struggle" has become the darling of those whom the Jewish left now see as "woke" visionaries of justice and mercy and enlightened thinking (Sanders, Cornell West, J Street, AOC and her Squad, the new socialist vanguard of university professors, etc.). What is a poor left/liberal Jew to do? Continue to hold tight to Zionism and have to share a space with Donald Trump, Pat Robertson, and Benjamin Netanyahu? No one will ever go out with them or invite them to fun parties! Or, maybe, just maybe, the better choice is to embrace a transformation to the newest and most "progressive" positions held by those they admire most! True, it means the abandonment of their long romance with the State of Israel. But, let's face it. The relationship was never that great. There were always problems. Those Israelis! So loud! So aggressive! Just not cool. A 2018 survey of young Jews in the San Francisco Bay Area found only 40% were "comfortable with a Jewish state and only a third sympathize more with Israel than Palestinians."
https://www.haaretz.com/us-news/.premium-vast-numbers-of-california-jews-disengaging-from-israel-survey-finds-1.5821675)

The only issues that may keep a few of the liberal/left Jews holding onto a tepid Zionism are:

1- Israel remains the only country in the Middle East that doesn't criminalize homosexuality (Tel Aviv is actually a gay haven of international renown).

2-Israel does have some great tech jobs (Facebook, Google, Apple, etc. are all onsite and hiring).

3-Israel remains the only Middle Eastern location a Jewish tourist can visit where much of the local population doesn't view them as members of a cruel and blasphemous people.

But even with these items in the plus column, siding with the Donald, Bibi, and those Holy Rollers is just not an acceptable option! Decision time has definitely arrived.

Trump's Romancing the (Jerusalem) Stone

Some marry for love. Others for money. A few marry because they find significant others that they hold in high esteem. And of course, not all marriages last. The question is why has President Trump "married" himself to Israel and Zionism? As I have written before, there is no denying that Trump has showered Israel with gifts the likes of which no other suitor has come close to matching. Need I list them again?

1- Moving the U.S. Embassy to Jerusalem

2- Cutting funding to the Palestinians in response to their non-cooperation with Israel

3-Agreeing with Netanyahu and withdrawing from the Iranian nuclear agreement

4-Taking the Palestinian state off the table as a requirement for American peace-brokering

5-Recognition of the Golan Heights as sovereign Israel

6-Not opposing Israel's annexation of West Bank territory

But what is the source of this infatuation? Will Trump be faithful, or is he a fickle lover who cannot be counted on when the going gets rough? As with all politicians, and most people, there is certainly an element of expediency to this love affair. President

Trump, with all his unpredictable, occasionally outrageous behavior, is constant in one way—he is careful not to upset what he sees as his base of support. This political instinct is highly ingrained and consistent in him for a man who has no previous political history. A major part of the Trump base consists of the Evangelicals, and they believe that Zionism is the prelude to their anticipated "Second Coming of the Messiah." Trump knows that this is VERY important to them—much more than the State of Israel is to most American Jews. He cannot do enough for Israel in that it shows that he is, in a way, "the Chosen One" to help bring about the Christian eschatological destiny.

So, as long as the Evangelicals love Israel and Zionism, Trump will too. I don't think this will change if Netanyahu is no longer prime minister, or if Israel and the U.S. have some other policy disagreements. There are bigger, more fundamental issues at play here that secure this connection. On the other hand, if, for some reason, the Evangelicals begin to see Zionism differently than they do now, then all bets are off. But that seems unlikely.

It doesn't hurt for Trump that Israel is also a shining example of the benefits of border security and the proud guardians of their national identity—two issues that are also quite important to the Trump base. But these items are seriously secondary to the previously stated Evangelical one. So, as Zionism has become a subcategory of Evangelicalism, the liberal Democrat Zionist is left out in the cold. Other than the Orthodox Jews, who also see Israel through a holy and messianic lens, the American Jew who previously included Zionism among his or her other list of identified values, is now not so sure. I fear we are at the cusp of a significant De-Zionation phenomenon that will further split the already fractured American Jewish community into highly defined pro and anti- Israel camps. The process of annexation of West Bank territory is certain to heighten this intra-community friction. Whether this process will be accelerated or slowed by a second

Trump term is difficult to know. On the one hand, with Trump continuing as president, Zionism would remain captured by Evangelicalism on the political front. And if a liberal/left candidate became commander in chief, it would raise the volume and influence of those who see Israel as an apartheid state that persecutes an indigenous, disenfranchised Palestinian people. Either way, the future of American Jewish community support of Israel is imperiled.

Chapter 17

Trump's Love of Walls
Holy and Unholy

Before I built a wall I'd ask to know
What I was walling in or walling out,
And to whom I was like to give offense.
Something there is that doesn't love a wall.
(from "Mending Wall" by Robert Frost)

There used to be a popular quiz show called *Password*. One player would be given a "secret word" and sit across from his or her partner player, who did not know the word. The player who knew the word would provide one-word clues to the second player, who would try to guess the "secret word" from these one-word clues. If you were playing this game today and you were given the word "wall," a pretty good one-word clue to give your partner would be "Trump." The building of "a big beautiful wall along the U.S. southern border which Mexico will pay for" was the issue that launched the unlikely presidential campaign of Donald Trump, and, to a significant degree, remains the defining issue of his unprecedented presidency.

American pundits and experts have been shocked by Trump in so many ways, and one of them was just how much the building of a security wall to prevent illegal southern immigration resonated with a significant percentage of the American electorate. Although many Republican candidates in 2016 brought up immigration in the wake of the 2015 Paris terrorist attack, it was only Donald Trump who made immigration the primary issue of his presidential campaign.

https://www.politico.com/story/2015/11/paris-attacks-republicans-immigration-trump-cruz-215895

Trump stated then, and continues to insist, that building the wall will significantly reduce an influx of criminals and illegal drugs. Trump's now infamous initial statement on the issue was made in June 2015 at the beginning of his campaign:

> When Mexico sends its people, they're not sending the best. They're sending people that have lots of problems and they're bringing those problems. They're bringing drugs, they're bringing crime. They're rapists and some, I assume, are good people, but I speak to border guards and they're telling us what we're getting.

Over three years later and well into the Trump presidency, in January 2019, Trump told reporters in the White House Rose Garden:

> Today, I'm announcing several critical actions that my administration is taking to confront a problem that we have right here at home…we are going to confront the national-security crisis on our southern border. And we are going to do it one way or the other. We have to do it. Not because it was a campaign promise, which it is—was one of many, by the way, not my only one…. But one of the things I said I have to do and I want to do is border security, because we have tremendous amounts of drugs flowing into our country, much of it coming from the southern border. When you look and when you listen to politicians, in

particular, certain Democrats, they say it all comes through the port of entry. It's wrong. It's wrong. It's just a lie. It's all a lie. They say walls don't work. Walls work 100 percent. You just take a look almost everywhere. Take a look at Israel. They are building another wall. Their wall is 99.9 percent effective, they told me. Ninety-nine-point-nine percent. That is what it would be with us, too. The only weakness is they go to the wall and go around the wall. They go around the wall and in, okay, that's what it is. It's very simple. And a big majority of the big drugs, the big drug loads don't go through ports of entry…. They go through areas where you have no wall. Everybody knows that. Nancy knows it. Chuck knows it. They all know it. It's all a big lie. It's a big con game. You don't have to be very smart to know, you put up a barrier, the people come in and—that's it, they can't do anything, unless they walk left or right and they find an area where there is no barrier and they come into the United States.

Although Trump's statement is rambling, his position is pretty clear. And with the 2020 presidential election fast approaching, Trump's unfulfilled promise from his 2016 campaign to build this wall is going to be a major political issue for him. This will intensify his efforts to build the wall, or at least make significant progress on it by November 2020. A recent *Vanity Fair* article cited a *Washington Post* report about Trump's determination to fulfill this campaign promise:

> The Washington Post reports that the president has "directed aides to fast-track billions of dollars" worth of construction contracts, aggressively seize private land, and disregard environmental rules, according to current and former officials involved with the project." In the coming weeks, Defense Secretary Mark Esper is expected to approve the White House's request to reroute $3.6 billion in Pentagon funds to the project, money that the president decided to divert from apparently less important Defense Department projects after lawmakers refused to pony up $5 billion. When staffers have nervously suggested that Trump's demands are unworkable or illegal, the president has apparently told them not to worry because he'll pardon everyone who helps him get this thing done, and has "waved off worries about contracting procedures and the use of eminent domain, saying 'take the land,'" according to officials who sat in on the

meetings. As a senior official told the Post, the companies contracted to build the fencing and access roads have been using "heavy earth-moving equipment" in "environmentally sensitive border areas adjacent to U.S. national parks and wildlife preserves," but, citing national security concerns, the administration has waived impact studies and standard procedural safeguards. "They don't care how much money is spent, whether landowners' rights are violated, whether the environment is damaged, the law, the regs, or even prudent business practices," the senior official said. (Asked for comment, an anonymous White House staffer told the Post that of course Trump is totally joking when he talks about pardoning people for breaking the law on his behalf).
https://www.vanityfair.com/news/2019/08/donald-trump-wall-pardons

The COVID-19 crisis has not stopped or even slowed Trump's determination to make significant progress on the southern border wall by the election. If anything, the pandemic has been absorbed into the Trump narrative of portraying the wall as a way to keep all people and things destructive from entering the U.S. from its southern border. Now you can add to this list those crossing over who are carrying the COVID-19 virus. A May 13, 2020 ABC News story by Quinn Owen stated:

> Construction on President Donald Trump's border wall continues undeterred amid the coronavirus pandemic, and while progress extending fortifications along the border is minimal, the impact of upgraded steel barricades is felt by both Border Patrol agents and environmental advocates. In meetings with U.S. Customs and Border Protection officials in the southwest, Secretary of Homeland Security Chad Wolf said the wall was more essential than ever in the fight against coronavirus. "It allows them to move resources to other areas of the border that are very difficult to control," Wolf told reporters Wednesday in Tucson, Arizona. Approximately 50 miles of barriers have been built since the end of February, when the first deaths linked to the coronavirus were reported in the U.S. That figure accounts for more than a quarter of all border wall construction completed under the Trump administration. https://www.yahoo.com/gma/border-wall-construction-plows-southwestern-us-undeterred-covid-211003137.html.

Trump may not be the most accurate or honest person in America, but there are a few things that he holds dear. One of these seems to be his campaign promises. He is *very* dedicated to keeping them. Perhaps he senses with his wily Trumpian instincts that the keeping of campaign promises will assure those who voted for him as the "non-politician" that he can be trusted to deliver. He refuses to be categorized as just another typical pol who stereotypically makes campaign promises, gets elected, and doesn't keep them. The question is whether Trump will be so dedicated to keeping this particular promise that he miscalculates and spends too much time, energy, and political capital on an issue that will not win him the 2020 race. Perhaps there are some good reasons that many successful politicians *don't* keep their campaign promises. Sometimes it is politically expedient not to keep them.

But it's not looking good for Trump's chances to fulfill this all-important southern border wall promise. He hasn't been able to make much significant progress and the cost estimates are quite astronomical. As of July 2019, U.S. Customs and Border Protection confirmed that, although they had begun to replace old fencing, no new wall had yet been built. About 60 miles of *replacement* wall has been completed since 2017. A private organization called "We Build the Wall" has also constructed three-quarters of a mile of new wall on private property near El Paso, Texas, with Trump's encouragement. During the period of February-May 2020, approximately 50 additional miles of new barrier have been completed. But the total length of the continental border with Mexico is 1,954 miles and there are only about 650 miles of fencing and barriers in place- approximately 600 miles of which were built many years before Trump's presidency.

Trump's administration did have a number of wall prototypes made in the fall of 2017. Estimates of the cost to actually complete the border wall vary greatly, ranging from $12-45 billion. Trump, during the 2016 campaign, estimated a $12 billion price tag, and Senate Majority Leader Mitch McConnell assessed the project at a slightly higher cost of $15 billion.

The Wall Is Now an Official "Emergency"
It's not that Trump has given up trying, and he is nothing if not determined. On February 15, 2019, Trump signed a bill to fund the government for the balance of the fiscal year, but derided the budget bill as inadequate because it contained only $1.375 billion for border security. Trump had earlier insisted he needed $5.7 billion to extend the Mexico–United States barrier. At the same time, Trump signed a declaration that the situation at the southern border constituted a national emergency. This declaration ostensibly made available $600 million from the Treasury Forfeiture Fund, $2.5 billion from the United States Department of Defense (including anti-drug accounts), and $3.6 billion from military construction accounts, for a total of $8 billion when added to the $1.375 billion allocated by Congress.

On February 27, 2019, the House of Representatives voted 245-182 in favor of a bill rejecting Trump's declaration of a national emergency on the southern border. On March 14, the Senate did the same on a vote of 59-41 (including all Democrats

and 12 Republicans). The next day, Trump vetoed the bill. It was the first veto of his presidency. Overriding his veto would have required a two-thirds majority in both houses of Congress. So, the emergency declaration stands.

In March 2019, the Pentagon issued a list of proposed military construction projects that could be postponed, under the president's emergency declaration, so that their funding could be used for the southern border wall. The Pentagon has authorized up to $1 billion to be transferred to the Army Corps of Engineers for construction of additional barriers. In the next month, the U.S. Border Patrol reported that 450 miles of wall is planned to be built by the end of 2020. If Trump really manages to get almost 500 miles of wall built by election day, he will be able to say he kept his promise. But the Democrats will do everything in their power to stop this progress and make a liar out of him. I wonder what the Las Vegas odds are for him getting his 450 miles done by election day?

Trump does have some alternative options. One is to give up on the wall for the 2020 election and heap blame on the Democrats. A second choice is to puff and spin the small amount of fence/wall work that has been done. But this won't be easy if there is nothing or almost nothing there. A wall is a solid visible edifice. It has a length and a height and is there (or not there) for all to see or not see. You can't say that it's built if it isn't. It's very hard to spin this one. It's not like a trade or economic policy or even a military strategy, which is much more long-term, visionary, and susceptible to spin. A wall is very concrete, so to speak.

Israel, Netanyahu, and the Wall
In January 2017 Israeli Prime Minister Netanyahu commented on Trump's desire to build a wall on the U.S.-Mexican border. The Jerusalem Post wrote:

> "President Trump is right," Netanyahu tweeted in a message that displayed an Israeli and an American flag. "I built a wall along Israel's southern border. It stopped all illegal immigration. Great success. Great idea," he added. The wall that Netanyahu is talking about is one along the Israeli border with Egypt which was completed six years ago (2011). According to experts like Dr. Ofer Israeli, a geostrategist and internal security policy expert who lectures at the Interdisciplinary Center in Herzliya, the barrier has been extremely effective and he stated that the quantity of human trafficking "is almost zero now." He also

claims that it has been very effective in defending Israel against terrorist attack from the Salafi-jihadists active in Egypt's Sinai Peninsula. Dr. Israeli also commented on the challenges of Trump's proposed wall. "The U.S. and Mexico are not hostile entities," said Israeli. "There is a wish to prevent human trafficking from Mexico, where Latin American migrants, as well as migrants from other countries, pour into. If they set up a significant obstacle that is high-quality with sensors, it will be extremely costly because the border is over 3,000 kilometers long." The great distances between the stations that monitor the barrier would mean that it would not be full-proof in stopping the migration flow, explained Israeli. "The question is whether the U.S. is willing to invest this huge sum."
https://www.jns.org/six-years-after-completion-israels-border-fence-with-egypt-has-transformed-the-south/

Israel also recently completed a border fence between southern Israel and Jordan. But perhaps Israel's most important and controversial wall is the 440-mile barrier built in the West Bank along the Green Line (the previous border of Israel and Jordan before the Six-Day War in which the West Bank area came under Israeli control). This barrier was built in the midst of the Second Intifada in September 2000 to stop the wave of terrorism inside Israel. The barrier is not without its own political ramifications. In 2003, the United Nations General Assembly adopted a resolution that stated the wall contradicts international law and should be removed; the vote was 144-4 with 12 abstentions.

The barrier has been highly effective. Suicide bombings have decreased dramatically. Al-Aqsa Martyrs' Brigades, Hamas, and the Palestinian Islamic Jihad have been less able to conduct many of their operations due to this boundary wall, preventing multiple attacks in Israel, decreasing in those areas where the barrier has been completed. The Israeli Ministry of Foreign Affairs reports that in 2002, there were 452 fatalities from terrorist attacks. Before the completion of the first continuous segment (July 2003) from the beginning of the Second Intifada, 73 Palestinian suicide bombings were carried which were found to have originated in the West

Bank, killing 293 Israelis and injuring over 1,900. After the completion of the first continuous segment through the end of 2006, there were 12 attacks based in the West Bank, killing 64 people and wounding 445. Attacks further declined in 2007 and 2008 to nine (a 98% reduction from the peak level) and continue to occur at this much-diminished level.

There's Something (Jewish) that Doesn't Love a Wall

Jews have many negative connotations associated with walls that have, perhaps, fueled the liberal Jewish majority's outrage at Trump's grand vision of a "great wall." Historically, Jews have been excluded from entering societies' mainstream by walls. More often, they've physically been "walled in" rather than "walled out." The word "ghetto" comes from Italian and describes the first walling in of a minority (the Jews) in 1516. Jewish ghettos existed in many European cities. More recently, the Nazis established ghettos for Jews and Romani people, whose inhabitants were then sent to concentration camps. The Russian Jews in the time of the Czars were cordoned off within the Pale of Settlement. The Jew, although thriving as an affluent participant in America, still has a strong identification with groups that are excluded, particularly by physical barriers, and this may be why Trump's wall project is so reviled by many on the left as a symbol of exclusion and intolerance.

Walls Holy and Unholy

For the Jewish people, the "Western Wall" (aka "Wailing Wall" aka the "Kotel") was originally erected as part of the expansion of the Second Temple in Jerusalem begun by Herod the Great, containing the steep hill of the Temple Mount, in a large rectangular structure topped by a huge flat platform, creating more space for the Temple itself and its buildings. As the remaining remnant of the Second Temple it is a site of great holiness for Jews who have been coming to it for centuries to pray and draw closer to God. Israel gained control of the Western Wall on June 10, 1967, following the Six-Day War. Brigadier Rabbi Shlomo Goren proclaimed after its capture that "Israel would never again relinquish the Wall," a stance supported by Israeli Minister for Defense Moshe Dayan and Chief of Staff General Yitzhak Rabin. Rabin described the moment Israeli soldiers reached the Wall:

> There was one moment in the Six-Day War which symbolized the great victory: that was the moment in which the first paratroopers—under Gur's command—reached the stones of the Western Wall, feeling the emotion of the place; there never was, and never will be, another moment like it. Nobody staged that moment. Nobody planned it in advance. Nobody prepared it and nobody was prepared for it; it was as if Providence had directed the whole thing: the paratroopers weeping—loudly and in pain— over their comrades who had fallen along the way, the words of the Kaddish prayer heard by Western Wall's stones after 19 years of silence, tears of mourning, shouts of joy, and the singing of "Hatikvah."
> https://mfa.gov.il/mfa/foreignpolicy/mfadocuments/yearbook 10/pages/address%20to%20the%20knesset%20by%20prime% 20minister%20rabin%20on%20jerusalem.aspx

On May 22, 2017, Trump became the first president to visit the Western Wall in Jerusalem. He was accompanied by his son-in-law and senior adviser Jared Kushner, who is an orthodox Jew,

and by Western Wall Rabbi Shmuel Rabinovich, First Lady Melania Trump, and Ivanka Trump, the president's daughter. She prayed at the Western Wall area reserved for women. This visit helped confirm Trump's unique support for the State of Israel.

For many of Trump's core supporters, the proposed southern wall with Mexico also has great meaning. To call it "holy" would be going a bit too far, but not by much. It is important to realize how much the idea of the southern border wall is wrapped up with many Americans' strong emotional connection to being citizens of these United States. There are a few ways, as an American citizen, to view this country. One is to appreciate it as a place whose government and resources allow an individual to thrive. Its freedoms and opportunities free me to utilize my talents to achieve success in many areas. But this perception of America, as primarily an efficient catalyst to individual and family achievement does not quite encompass what some would believe to be true American patriotism.

For many who form the hardcore base of Trump's constituency and fervently cheer at his rallies, America is not just a well-functioning means to success and personal freedom. Being an American is much more than this to them. It is an essential part of their personal identity and pride. The great history and accomplishment of the United States are their accomplishments. It goes far beyond the quality of life benefits that come from citizenship. True "Trumpsters" who resonated so strongly to the southern wall issue are not dedicated to Trump's wall merely because they think it will improve their job prospects or lower crime and drugs.

Even if the employment and crime issues are taken out of the equation it would not change their perspective. This is because they see the illegal immigrants entering and benefiting from the

country as an insult to their own cherished identity as American citizens and as a besmirching of the stature of what it means to be an American. If you're not a member of the club you can't just sneak in the door and use all the clubhouse facilities and pretend to be a member! If you could, what does it mean to actually *be* a member? As someone once said, what makes a club a club is not so much the people in it as much as the people who are *not* allowed in it. To some extent, what makes a country a country is that not everyone can be part of it.

This was succinctly expressed by Trump when discussing the illegal immigrant issue. He famously stated, "They have to go. We either have a country or we don't have a country." Republican Steve King of Iowa, who is viewed by many as being more extreme in his outspokenness on nationalism than the president, captured the almost religious fervor with which many revile illegal immigration as a violation of everything American. King wrote an article for Breitbart in 2017 that expressed this idea that allowing illegal immigration represents the destruction of what it means to be an American. He wrote:

> During the campaign, President Trump made an unforgettable appearance in Des Moines, Iowa…. What I remember was a solemn promise that then-candidate Donald Trump made to the American people. When asked by NBC's Chuck Todd what he would do about illegal aliens amnestied under the DACA program, Donald Trump minced no words: "They have to go," he said. "Chuck, we either have a country or we don't have a country." With this one phrase, Candidate Trump distilled the crux of the matter into an argument everyone understands. "We either have a country or we don't have a country" is exactly right. We are either a nation defined by its borders, its culture, and its adherence to the Rule of Law or we aren't. We either recognize that United States citizenship is intrinsically meaningful, or it isn't. We either place America and Americans First, or we don't. https://www.breitbart.com/politics/2017/08/30/exclusive-steve-king-we-either-have-a- country-or-we-dont/

This issue is not going away. Even if the economy remains robust and crime low, the drumbeat of "build the wall" will continue to resonate loudly with Trump's energized base. And make no mistake: President Trump is listening very carefully, and will do his utmost to get it built—even if Mexico doesn't pay for it.

Chapter 18
Trump's Hyper-Masculinity Versus the Jewish Feminist Mystique

The premise of this chapter, which you may or may not agree with, is that there are identifiable masculine and feminine qualities, and that they often translate into individual and political party positions. Some hold that the whole concept of masculine and feminine traits is specious and the result of cultural biases. I am starting from the point of view that there are typically masculine and feminine traits and that these traits impact political positions more common in each of the genders, with the Democrats being favored by women and men who value typically feminine traits, and the Republicans favored by men and those women who value typically masculine traits. Although President Trump is not your typical Republican, as a prototypical alpha male, he does appeal to the masculine leanings of many Republican Party members.

Every person, regardless of his or her gender, has both a masculine and feminine character that combine to form each individual's personality. Typical masculine characteristics, in my opinion, are those that focus on power, dominance, and aggressive action. Masculine political views often reflect this power focus by giving priority to individual freedoms and aggressive domestic and foreign policies. These include attacking an enemy, aggressive drilling and mining of natural resources, intensive land development, tough criminal law, reducing government taxes and regulations on individuals or businesses, and the right to bear arms. Feminine issues are those that focus on nurturing, cooperation, and protection of the vulnerable. These translate into policies focused on helping the poor, the procuring of basic physical needs for all, and the management of competition to protect the weaker and more vulnerable (social service programs, government protections for disabled individuals, highly regulated economic policies and stricter environmental protection laws).

Clearly, these typically masculine characteristics are not limited to men, nor the feminine character to women, although the terms derive from what has historically been most common to each gender. There are men who have a highly nurturing, compassionate nature and women who are focused on power, passionate about individual freedom, and favor bold military policies. There have been women government leaders who reflected what might be termed a masculine agenda (Elizabeth I of England and Margaret Thatcher both come to mind), as well as male leaders who reflected a feminine agenda (Bill Clinton's famous "I feel your pain," as an example).

A greater percentage of women than men identify themselves as Democrats. Voter analysis of the 2018 midterm elections found that 51% of men voted Republican and 47% Democrat. Among women 59% voted Democrat and 40% Republican. Total black voters (men and women) favored Democrats to Republicans 90%

to 9%, reducing what would be an even more dramatic difference between the genders. These trends have been fairly consistent for decades. Although the difference is significant, it is very far from a clean gender breakdown by party. Also, regardless of one's personal feelings, sometimes a person chooses a political party for practical or ideological reasons that don't reflect one's personal "gut" feelings about issues. For example, a man or woman who might otherwise embrace Republican Party ideals may identify and vote Democrat due to a union job or a family immigration issue. Similarly, a person more Democratic by nature may vote Republican to lower his taxes or help her small business. Also, many people may feel one way emotionally, but conclude that an agenda different from their personal feelings is best for the country at the time.

Trumpian Hyper-Masculinity

There is no doubt that Donald Trump portrays many stereotypically masculine characteristics (some might label them "toxic male traits"). The following come to mind:

1-Trump the "playboy." Heterosexually promiscuous with a valuing of feminine sexual beauty. There is no need to go into details here. The first lady was "Miss World" and there is Stormy Daniels, Karen McDougal, and his famed affair with Marla Maples in the '90s. He is, perhaps, America's most famous "lady's man." This is an often-overlooked reason for Trump's appeal to much of his base—both men and women. This attraction may seem unlikely or even unbelievable to those who are appalled by Trump's brusqueness and bravado, but there are many who are attracted to what they view as toughness and great strength.

2-Aggressiveness in business and political dealings with a love of winning. Here too Trump is iconic. *The Art of the Deal* was a runaway bestseller, and *The Apprentice* was also a "huge" hit. Both established Trump as the aggressive deal-maker and predatory, fearsome "boss of bosses."

3-Often in viscous attack mode against his detractors. I recall being shocked at the first Republican debate when Trump was asked by Fox News host and debate moderator Megyn Kelly about his use of language like "fat pigs," "dogs," "slobs," and "disgusting animals" to describe some women. The Donald didn't miss a beat. "Only Rosie O'Donnell," he interjected, generating gasps, applause, and laughter from the crowd. Then, of course, there are the disparaging monikers he invents and repeats about his opponents who he regularly attacks with his ubiquitous tweets. (See if you know who each one applies to!)

·Sleepy Joe

·Lyin' Hillary

·Lyin' Ted

·Crazy Nancy

·Little Marco

·Crazy Bernie

·Pencil Neck

·Pocahontas

He is "the attacker in chief" and has established his reputation as a ferocious opponent who will "give worse than he gets" to those who dare oppose him. Perhaps his most effective modicum has been the "fake news" tag he has used to undermine the credibility of many American news organizations. This too "has stuck" and become part of the American consciousness and public discourse.

4-Valuing power and domination. A *Psychology Today* article titled "Donald Trump's Values" by Ryne A. Sherman, PhD stated:

> Finally, when we combine this with Mr. Trump's low Altruism and high Tradition, the result is an individual who is—quite frankly—interested in dominance. Mr. Trump likes to be in charge of others, wants everyone to know he is in charge, has little sympathy for those who are unsuccessful, and prefers to maintain the current social hierarchy. As someone in charge, Mr.

Trump places a heavy emphasis on look and feel and will tend to make decisions based on gut reactions, with very little interest in what science and/or data may suggest.... Mr. Trump will have little tolerance for insubordination and criticism. As a result, he will surround himself with "yes men" either intentionally or unintentionally by alienating and firing anyone who does not support him or his ideas.

https://www.psychologytoday.com/us/blog/the-situation-lab/201603/donald-trumps-values

5-Territorial. Those tall buildings with "TRUMP" emblazoned on them: There's the Trump Towers he has built throughout the world, the Trump International Hotels and Trump Plazas. The president loves to build big, tall edifices with his name on them. This is of course a business decision, as it burnishes his brand, but it is also an expression of power and dominance. Trump's efforts do remind one of the Tower of Babel, in which the builders sought to "make a name for themselves." Trump literally places his name on his towers to "make a name for himself."

But I am stating the obvious. Whether or not you believe that deep down Trump is a scared, insecure little boy, or pretty much the same person he is on the outside, his behaviors and decisions reflect the masculine perspective. This "he-man" profile has not gone unnoticed by Trump's detractors, who see him as not just male, or hyper-male, but as the poster child for the "toxic male," which is viewed as a destructive natural force. In a 2016 *New York Magazine* article, "How Trump Has Revived the Republican Cult of Manliness," writer Jonathan Chait mused about the then candidate Trump's tapping into this "male toxicity":

The restoration of male authority threatened by social change is a central theme of Trump's candidacy. His business ventures had long ago identified specifically masculine luxuries—golf, steaks— as ripe for identification with the Trump brand. During the campaign, Trump has called for the statue of Joe Paterno, the legendary, disgraced Penn State coach who ignored evidence his defensive coordinator had serially raped young boys, to be restored to the place of honor from which it had been removed.

He campaigned in Indiana with Bobby Knight, who was fired as Indiana's basketball coach after years of misogynistic bullying. Trump's speeches invariably praise the police and decry complaints about excesses of enforcement. These other, threatened men of power are stand-ins for Trump's view of himself. Nothing enrages him more predictably than being challenged by a woman. He belittled Megyn Kelly as menstrual, and Carly Fiorina as ugly—the same treatment he doled out over the years to critics like Arianna Huffington, Rosie O'Donnell, and others. Trump has accused Clinton of owing her career to being a woman.
http://nymag.com/betamale/2016/05/gop-cult-masculinity-trump.html

A similar jaundiced view of Trump is expressed by James Hamblin in the *Atlantic* article "Trump Is a Climax of American Masculinity." He writes:

> Trump is in many other ways a caricature of a *man's man*. He shouts and bullies and berates people. He speaks mostly in superlatives and mentions himself in most sentences. He plays golf and has a head full of hair, as men are supposed to. He hasn't gone full Putin and hunted shirtless on horseback with his press pool, but he has alluded to the size of his penis from the stage of a presidential primary debate. Trump is a man who has demonstrated a propensity to fill the major cities of the world with enormous phalluses bearing his name.
> https://www.theatlantic.com/health/archive/2016/08/trump-masculinity-problem/494582/

These pundits portray Trump's masculinity with disdain and as a form of buffoonery. But whether you see it in this negative light or not, it is not politically insignificant. I would conclude, on the contrary, that this particularly Trumpian trait was key in his election as president of the United States. Perhaps more than any other trait, this hyper-masculinity energized and was embraced by the Trump base of white working-class men (and *many* from outside of that core group). Journalist Steven Watts, in the February 2017 article "Trump, JFK and the Masculine Mystique," is, in my opinion, close to the mark when he writes:

Many liberals and conservatives alike, with considerable reason, denounced Donald Trump as a policy ignoramus and mocked his simplistic, rambling statements on immigration, social issues, government regulation, and foreign policy. What they missed, however, was Trump's compelling connection to the cultural values—those fears, yearnings, and visions of vast swathes of the American voting public.

In this regard, Trump bears an interesting resemblance to an earlier president who in many ways created the template for modern holders of that office: John F. Kennedy. While quite different in terms of their *political* views, JFK and Trump can be seen as *cultural* phenomena, and they both energized great portions of the voting public in their respective eras. For example, both men demonstrated a striking celebrity appeal that was tailor-made for a modern American culture that has made entertainment, leisure, and self-fulfillment (as opposed to self-control) keys to achieving happiness and success. Kennedy and Trump also ascended politically through a mastery of another key factor in modern culture: communications technology. The former demonstrated his skill with the then-fresh medium of television while the latter has displayed mastery of new social-media technologies.

But perhaps the most subtle, yet powerful, cultural appeal of Kennedy and Trump came from their skillful deployment of a masculine mystique. These two candidates, in their own way, projected a strong male persona that resonated with underlying cultural concerns in America. Each moved center stage as an assertive masculine figure who appealed to mainstream Americans yearning for leadership by such a man. Their manly image, as much as their words, promised to allay deep-seated anxieties about masculine effectiveness in the modern world.

In a bold intellectual move, Watts draws close parallels between Trump and John F. Kennedy, as well as the U.S. society of the late '50s and that of our day. In both cases, masculinity was perceived by many men (and women) as being under attack and in decline. In Kennedy's case by the growing bureaucratic nature of business, and in Trump's case by the rise of feminism and the toxic perspective widely held by the highly educated regarding many characteristically masculine traits. Watts writes about the threat to masculinity in Kennedy's time:

> Kennedy rose to prominence and power over the last half of the 1950s, a time when there was a growing despair about the condition of American men. A mounting chorus of complaints blamed the vast growth of bureaucracy for reducing men to desk-bound, corpulent drones. Suburbanization supposedly trapped men in cul-de-sacs of consumer abundance and softened them as they changed diapers, orchestrated backyard barbecues, and watched television slumped in their easy chairs. Other critics claimed that growing numbers of women in the post-war workplace emasculated men; wives who took jobs captured the traditional male prerogative of being the breadwinner. *Look* magazine's gloomy three-part series on "The Decline of the American Male" concluded, "He is no longer the masculine, strong-minded man who pioneered the continent and built

> America's greatness." A 1958 *Esquire* essay entitled "The Crisis of Masculinity" summarized, "Today men are more and more conscious of maleness not as a fact but as a problem.".... Trump also has been raised to prominence and power, at least partly, by a great spasm of cultural anxiety about masculine decline in modern America. In recent years, a series of controversies has called into question long-accepted ideas about gender and sexuality, particularly on the male front. We've seen a recent vogue for transgender matters, such as the lionizing of Caitlyn (né Bruce) Jenner; the "bathroom wars," in which activists insist that biological men have the "right" to use women's toilet facilities and locker rooms; and the normalizing of gender "identifying," wherein individuals supposedly can choose any sexual identity they desire. Among many Americans, this trend has caused head-shaking over social standards.... At universities, denunciations of 'toxic masculinity' and 'male privilege' have become curricular rituals, and gender-bending initiatives are common. On the education front in recent years, legions of ordinary Americans have grown distressed by a string of developments regarding gender sensitivity. At the K–12 level, as Christina Hoff Sommers has detailed in *The War against Boys*, typically rambunctious seven-year-olds have been suspended for picking up a pencil and using it to shoot bad guys" while playing, and traditional games such

as dodge ball and red rover have been abolished for being too violent and destructive of self-esteem. At universities, denunciations of "toxic masculinity" and "male privilege" have become circular rituals.
https://www.nationalreview.com/2017/02/donald-trump-jfk-masculine- mystique/

As is often the case, intelligent people tend to underestimate the power of those aspects of the personality that are not often expressed. I believe that many if not most men are conflicted regarding the rapid changes in gender roles. Even those who outwardly convince others and themselves of their embrace of the new normal are threatened by the contemporary view that many of the traits that men had previously taken pride in are now viewed as flaws. This perspective is not limited to white working-class males. It's just that they are more comfortable expressing their distress and disdain regarding it. Most men cannot blithely reconstruct their long-held masculine self-image. Can someone so easily re-categorize qualities that were previously viewed as strengths as now being destructive, obsolete characteristics that now must be extinguished? For many, Trump is something of a savior as they drown in a sea of anti-masculinist values that have flooded every area of society. And like any drowning person, one is not too particular about the lifeline being thrown to him.

The Jewish Feminine Mystique

There are strong feminist elements in the American Jewish community, and many of the mid-20th century leaders in the feminist movement were Jewish. Betty Freidan was a leading figure in the women's movement in the United States. Her 1963 book *The Feminine Mystique* is often credited with sparking the second wave of American feminism in the 1960s and 1970s. Whereas first-wave feminism focused mainly on the issues of suffrage and overturning legal obstacles to gender such as voting rights and property rights, second-wave feminism broadened the debate to include sexuality, family, the workplace, and reproductive rights, along with official legal inequalities. In 1966, Friedan co-founded and was elected the first president of the National Organization for Women (NOW), which aimed to bring women "into the mainstream of American society now [in] fully equal partnership with men." Friedan was born Bettye Naomi Goldstein on February 4, 1921, in Peoria, Illinois, to Harry and Miriam (Horwitz) Goldstein, whose Jewish families were from Russia and Hungary.

In a May 2019 review by Roselyn Bell of Joyce Antler's recent book *Jewish Radical Feminism: Voices from the Women's Liberation Movement*, she writes:

> It was the elephant in the room: One couldn't help noticing that among the leaders of the second-wave feminist movement of the late 1960s and early 1970s, a large proportion were Jewish. …For example, among the 12 founders of the Boston Women's Health Book Collective, which published the *Our Bodies, Ourselves* series, eight were Jewish—but their Jewishness went unremarked until much later. Joyce Antler, professor emerita of American Jewish history and culture at Brandeis University, wondered why the Jewish component of these women's identities had received so little attention. In 2011, she convened a conference on "Women's Liberation and Jewish Identity," bringing together some 40 activists in the general women's liberation movement or in the feminist movement within Judaism. Out of that conference came this book, which delves into the life stories of these participants and the many faces of Jewish feminism. Some, such as the members of the Boston Women's Health Book Collective, found that their feminism was informed by their Judaism, and so, for instance, they celebrated seders together for many years.
>
> Others, like Arlene Agus, co-founder in 1971 of Ezrat Nashim, the first American Jewish feminist organization, and Blu Greenberg, who went on to found the Jewish Orthodox Feminist Alliance in 1997, were deeply knowledgeable Jews who began to challenge the patriarchy and sexism of Jewish religious life. …The battles to be fought varied from religious movement to movement, but the women whom Antler calls "identified Jewish feminists" changed Judaism itself over the next 45 years. They became rabbis and cantors, rediscovered Rosh Hodesh as a

women's holiday, wrote new prayer books, created feminist seders and challenged the male-dominated Jewish establishment. https://www.hadassahmagazine.org/author/roselyn-bell/

Presently, U.S. Supreme Court Justice Ruth Bader Ginsberg is a highly prominent Jewish woman who is identified by many as a hero of American feminism. She was born and grew up in Flatbush, Brooklyn. Her father was a Jewish immigrant from Odessa, Ukraine, and her mother was born in New York to Austrian Jewish parents. The Bader family belonged to East Midwood Jewish Center, a Conservative synagogue, where Ruth learned tenets of the Jewish faith and gained familiarity with Hebrew. At age 13, Ruth acted as "camp rabbi" at a Jewish summer program at Camp Che-Na-Wah in Minerva, New York.

In March 2015, Ginsburg and Rabbi Lauren Holtzblatt released "The Heroic and Visionary Women of Passover," an essay highlighting the roles of five key women in the saga: "These women had a vision leading out of the darkness shrouding their world. They were women of action, prepared to defy authority to make their vision a reality bathed in the light of the day." In addition, she decorates her chambers with an artist's rendering of the Hebrew phrase from Deuteronomy, "*Zedek, zedek, tirdof,*" ("Justice, justice shall you pursue") as a reminder of her heritage and professional responsibility.

In September 2019 Justice Ginsburg accepted *Moment Magazine*'s inaugural Human Rights Award. *Moment* is a magazine that focuses on the American Jewish community. It was founded in 1975 by Nobel Prize laureate Elie Wiesel and Jewish activist Leonard Fein. Speaking of her own "heroes," she mentioned Hadassah founder Henrietta Szold and Emma Lazarus, the poet of "Statue of Liberty" fame and a strong Zionist.

Although, traditionally, Judaism limits political and religious leadership to men, there are foundations of Jewish law and practice that, one could argue, provide a "launching pad" for modern feminism. Although these elements may not seem like much from a modern perspective, in ancient times they were quite unique. For example:

1- Jewish law allowed women to own property and sue in court.

2- Women had to personally consent to a marriage union—it could not be imposed upon them by their parents.

3- Women had a right to divorce their husbands, and a man had to financially provide for a woman if he divorced her.

4- Women had equal status under the law regarding protection from theft, murder, or other crimes.

5- Some women were prophets -the highest spiritual level.

6- The fore-mothers (Sarah, Rivkah, Leah, and Rachel) played key roles in the development of the Jewish people.

7- A wife had to be treated with gentleness, consideration and respect by her husband.

Flash forward to more recent times, and feminism has had a profound impact on organized Jewish life with much of the rabbinic and organizational leadership in Conservative and Reform Judaism being filled by women. Even the Orthodox community, though not ordaining women rabbis, has established positions of increased authority in deciding Jewish law and playing greater leadership roles in orthodox Jewish organizations. There are also many prominent orthodox Jewish feminist organizations, including the Jewish Orthodox Feminist Alliance (JOFA). On the JOFA website (www.jofa.org) under "About Us" it states:

> JOFA, the Jewish Orthodox Feminist Alliance, expands the spiritual, ritual, intellectual and political opportunities for women within the framework of halakha (Jewish law), by advocating meaningful participation and equality for women in family life, synagogues, houses of learning and Jewish communal organizations to the full extent possible within halakha.

Trump: Feminist Public Enemy #1 and Masculinist Hero

Donald Trump is considered as something of an *arch*-enemy of feminists, Jewish or otherwise. The more strident one's feminist position, the more intense the opposition to the president. Ironically, though predictably, Trump has singlehandedly done what thousands of hard-working feminists have been unable to do—he has revitalized the feminist movement to an unprecedented level. A July 2017 CNN article, "Donald Trump is the Best and Worst Thing That's Happened to Modern American Feminism," by Jodi Enda, stated:

> Debate all you want whether Donald Trump is bad for women, but there's no disputing this: He is great for the women's movement. The election of a president whom detractors view as misogynistic and backward-thinking has done nothing less than spark a wholesale resurgence of feminism. His defeat of the first woman who might have been president—coupled with his incendiary comments about women and his divisive policies on
>
> reproductive rights and other issues—lit a fire under a movement that had failed to excite younger generations of women who benefited from the battles of the last century and saw no need to keep fighting. They do now. "There's never been anything like this," says Eleanor Smeal, president of the Feminist Majority Foundation and a veteran leader of the women's movement. "I believe the culture has dramatically changed." In more than 50 interviews since Inauguration Day, leaders of legacy and upstart women's groups as well as experienced and newly minted activists have told me about a grassroots effort that could dwarf the crusades—if not the results—of earlier years. Previous campaigns garnered huge gains for women, most notably suffrage, employment and reproductive rights. In the age of Trump, the movement is not fixated on one isolated goal, but on a combination of causes that begins, first and foremost, with preventing a Republican president and Congress from curtailing existing rights.
> https://www.cnn.com/interactive/2017/politics/state/womens-movement-donald-trump/

Conclusion

Is the "Great Trump Divide" in the Jewish and general community in part due to the discomfort some are experiencing with regards to changing gender identities? Are Jewish women who have been among the leaders of the feminist movement, particularly irked by Trump's archaic "he-man" persona? I think so. This underlying conflict which has been simmering for some time has been brought to a boil by Trumps "toxic male" persona and intensified by the energies of other brewing conflicts (rich versus not rich, black versus white, capitalists versus socialists, industrialists versus environmentalists, young versus old, etc.) But to ignore the gender issue would be to miss a key ingredient in this potent political stew.

Some might say that Trump is a force that has been brought about by the overreach of an opposing force—that transformations in gender identity in U.S. society have gone so far so fast that many men (and some women) are uneasy with the new reality that demonizes feelings and behaviors the were raised to respect. They look to Trump to "put on the brakes" on a trend that has accelerated at a rate that frightens and disorients them, though this underlying gender conflict is usually ignored and the conflict between genders portrayed as being based on loftier ethical and political issues (justice, individual rights, freedom, economics).

But in the privacy of the voting booth, a few months from now, I believe many will pull the lever for Trump as a vote not so much for him, but for the rapidly fading image of "the American male" who they look back on, for better or worse, with a degree of fondness and nostalgia.

Chapter 19

Will Trump's Impeachment Be Blamed on the Jews?

The impeachment of President Trump will remain in our consciousness for quite some time to come and will play a significant role in the 2020 presidential campaign. The core event upon which the impeachment investigation centered was the July 25, 2019 call from President Trump to Ukrainian President Volodymyr Zelensky. The following are excerpts from the official transcript of the call created from notes and released by the White House:

> President Zelensky: ...I would also like to thank you for your great support in the area of defense. We are ready to continue to cooperate for the next steps, specifically we are almost ready to buy more Javelins from the United States for defense purposes.

> The President: I would like you to do us a favor though because our country has been through a lot and Ukraine knows a lot about

it. I would like you to find out what happened with this whole situation with Ukraine, they say Crowdstrike.... I guess you have one of your wealthy people.... The server, they say Ukraine has it. There are a lot of things that went on, the whole situation.... I think you are surrounding yourself with some of the same people. I would like to have the Attorney General call you or your people and I would like you to get to the bottom of it. As you said yesterday, that whole nonsense ended with a very poor performance by a man named Robert Mueller, an incompetent performance, but they say a lot of it started with Ukraine. Whatever you can do, it's very important that you do it if that's possible.

President Zelensky: We are great friends and you Mr. President have friends in our country so we can continue our strategic partnership. I also plan to surround myself with great people and in addition to that investigation, I guarantee as the President of Ukraine that all the investigations will be done openly and candidly. That I can assure you

The President: Good because I heard you had a prosecutor who was very good and he was shut down and that's really unfair. A lot of people are talking about that, the way they shut your very good prosecutor down and you had some very bad people involved. Mr. Giuliani is a highly respected man. He was the mayor of New York City, a great mayor, and I would like him to call you. I will ask him to call you along with the Attorney General. Rudy very much knows what's happening and he is a very capable guy. If you could speak to him that would be great. The former ambassador from the United States, the woman, was bad news and the people she was dealing with in the Ukraine were bad news so I just want to let you know that. The other thing, there's a lot of talk about Biden's son, that Biden stopped the prosecution and a lot of people want to find out about that so whatever you can do with the Attorney General would be great. Biden went around bragging that he stopped the prosecution so if you can look into it.... It sounds horrible to me.

The issue around which the congressional impeachment inquiry revolved was the intent of Trump in his request for Zelensky to investigate Biden's son's activities as a board member of the

Ukrainian energy company Burisma, and then Vice President Biden's role in pressuring the Ukrainian government to

remove their prosecutor, Viktor Shokin, who had previously led an investigation into Burisma's owners. In March 2016, then Vice President Biden requested that the Ukrainian government remove Shokin. Biden was representing the official position of the U.S. government, a position that was also supported by other Western governments and many in Ukraine, who accused Shokin of actually being soft on corruption. Also, to a lesser extent, the impeachment inquiry is focused on Trump's request for Zelensky to look into Crowdstrike, which Trump suspected of having access to Hillary Clinton's private server, or its contents, that were at the center of the Clinton email investigation by former FBI Director James Comey. In addition, in the Trump/Zelensky phone call Trump appears to some to be making Zelensky's invitation to the White House at some future date contingent on carrying out these investigations:

> The President: Good. Well, thank you very much and I appreciate that. I will tell Rudy and Attorney General Barr to call. Thank you. Whenever you would like to come to the White House, feel free to call. Give us a date and we'll work that out. I look forward to seeing you.

> President Zelenskyy: Thank you very much. I would be very happy to come and would be happy to meet with you personally and get to know you better.

The full transcript of the call between Trump and Zelensky can be found at: https://time.com/5685947/trump-ukraine-call/

Was Trump using his power as president to pressure Zelensky into assisting him with finding information that would be damaging to Trump's potential 2020 presidential opponent, Joe Biden? Biden was the clear front-runner to win the Democratic Party nomination at the time of the call and has solidified that position. But even if Trump did make the $400 million in congressionally sanctioned military aid contingent on these investigations, was a crime committed? Randall D. Eliaon's September 23, 2019 *Washington Post* article, "If the Ukraine allegations are true, there are criminal consequences," states:

> The statute most directly relevant to the president's conduct is the federal bribery statute. Under 18 U.S.C. 201, it is a crime for a public official to (directly or indirectly) corruptly demand, seek, receive, or accept, or agree to receive or accept "anything of value" in return for being influenced in the performance of an official act. Trump is a public official under this statute. The official act would be his release of the military assistance to Ukraine. And the thing of value promised in return would be Ukraine agreeing to look for dirt on one of the president's top political rivals. (In bribery law, "anything of value" includes intangibles with subjective value to the official; creating damaging information on a key opponent would qualify.) The key issue would be proof of a quid pro quo. The official must agree to be influenced in exchange for the benefit and must have corrupt intent—the wrongful purpose to act out of self-interest rather than in the public interest. The whistleblower report allegedly was prompted by a "promise" made by the president to the Ukrainian leader. If such a promise related to releasing the U.S. aid in return for the Biden investigation, that could be crucial evidence of a quid pro quo. Such agreements need not be stated in express terms; corrupt actors are seldom so clumsy, and the law may not be evaded through winks and nods. Prosecutors often prove tacit agreements through circumstantial evidence including the timing of events and actions of the parties— and the timing here certainly looks suspicious. It also wouldn't matter if the administration ultimately relented in the face of congressional scrutiny and released the funds without a deal. In a bribery case, the crime is the demand for a quid pro quo, whether or not it succeeds.

The dial of whether there was a quid pro quo between Trump and Zelensky was significantly moved toward "yes" by the testimony of William B. Taylor Jr., the current U.S. chargé d'affaires to Ukraine. According to an October 22, 2019 *Washington Post* article, "5 takeaways from William Taylor's lengthy opening statement," by Aaron Blake:

> Taylor provides perhaps the most compelling evidence yet that this quid pro quo didn't just exist but was explicitly communicated to Ukraine. Taylor said he was told by National Security Council aide Tim Morrison that Sondland, the (U.S.) ambassador to the European Union, directly communicated that quid pro quo to a top Zelensky aide, Andriy Yermak. "During this same phone call, I had with Mr. Morrison, he went on to describe a conversation Ambassador Sondland had with Mr. Yermak at [a meeting in] Warsaw," Taylor said. "Ambassador Sondland told Mr. Yermak that the security assistance money would not come until President Zelensky committed to pursue the Burisma investigation." That's about as explicit as it gets—although it's secondhand. It appears that Morrison's testimony will now be key. Taylor also said Sondland later told him directly that both a meeting and military aid depended on the investigation.
> https://www.washingtonpost.com/politics/2019/10/22/takeawa ys-bill-taylors- crucial-opening-statement/

The conclusion of a quid pro quo was also strengthened by two unexpected sources—Tim Mulvaney, the acting White House chief of staff, and President Trump himself! Mulvaney, at an October 17, 2019 news conference held to explain Trump's decision to hold the upcoming G7 conference at the Trump National Doral in Miami, veered off-topic when he responded to a journalist's question. ABC News described Mulvaney's presentation as follows:

> Mulvaney had recounted that the president told him he didn't want to send Ukraine "a bunch of money and have them waste it, and have them spend it, have them use it to line their own pockets."
> "Those were the driving factors," Mulvaney said. "Did he also

mention to me in the past that the corruption related to the DNC server? Absolutely, no question about that. But that's it and that's why we held up the money." "So, the demand for an investigation into the Democrats was part of the reason that he ordered you to withhold funding to Ukraine?" Karl asked. "The look back to what happened in 2016 certainly was part of the thing that he was worried about in corruption with the nation," Mulvaney said. "And that is absolutely equivalent." "What you described is a quid pro quo," Karl pressed. "It is: Funding will not flow unless the investigation into the Democrats' server happens as well." "We do that all the time with foreign policy," Mulvaney answered. "We were holding up money at the same time for, what was it? The Northern Triangle countries. We were holding up aid at the Northern Triangle countries so that they—so that they would change their policies on immigration."

Hours later the White House and Mulvaney "walked back" the statement:

Once again, the media has decided to misconstrue my comments to advance a biased and political witch hunt against President Trump. Let me be clear, there was absolutely no quid pro quo between Ukrainian military aid and any investigation into the 2016 election. The president never told me to withhold any money until the Ukrainians did anything related to the server. The only reasons we were holding the money was because of concern about lack of support from other nations and concerns over corruption.

Perhaps even more surprising was Trump's own statement on October 3, 2019, in front of the White House, when he said:

China should start an investigation into the Bidens, because what happened in China is just about as bad as what happened with Ukraine. So, I would say that President Zelensky, if it were me, I would recommend that they start an investigation into the Bidens.

Hunter Biden was on the board of BHR (Shanghai) Equity Investment Fund Management Co., a business in China. (His intent was to step down from that position by October 31, 2019, according to his attorney, George Mesires.)

Whether these statements by Mulvaney and Trump were spontaneous, self-inflicted wounds, or some clever plan to desensitize the public to the idea of quid pro quo being an impeachable act, is unclear to me. Many have speculated on whether Trump may be acclimating the country to the idea that these activities, even if they were quid pro quo were not illegal or unusual. Others view Trump and his team's responses as being disorganized, inconsistent, and poorly executed.

The Jewish Connection to the Trump Impeachment

The percentage of people who thought that Trump should have been impeached and removed from office remained at about 50% (as of early October 2019). But, as most people know, although it takes a simple majority of the House of Representatives to impeach a president (218 votes out of the 435 members of the House of Representatives), it requires two-thirds of the Senate to then vote to remove him from office. So, with 235 Democratic members of the House, impeachment was certainly politically possible and it was carried out. However, two-thirds of the Senate (67 of the 100 senators) would have been needed to vote to "convict" Trump in order to remove him from office. There were only 49 Democratic senators. This means that 18 Republican senators would have had to vote to remove him. Polls during the Senate trial showed that Trump's approval rating among registered Republicans hovered near 90%, making a Senate conviction of the president unrealistic, if not impossible.

But did Trump's impeachment by the House and acquittal by the Senate have any lasting ramifications for the Jewish community? An October 20, 2019 *Jerusalem Post* article, "Jewish Democrats Express Support of Impeachment Inquiry Against Trump," by

Omri Nahmias stated:

> The Jewish Democratic Council of America (JDCA) expressed its support regarding a formal impeachment inquiry against US President Donald Trump, after House of Representatives Speaker

Nancy Pelosi announced on Tuesday that the chamber would open up the inquiry. "The Democratic-controlled House will examine whether Trump sought Ukraine's help to smear former vice president Joe Biden, the front-runner for the 2020 Democratic

presidential nomination. JDCA executive director Halie Soifer said in a statement that the decision by the Democratic leaders is "consistent with the US Constitution and essential for the future of our democracy." "[Trump] acted with impunity in flagrant disregard of the rule of law and his oath of office," Soifer said. "He has consistently acted to further his own political and personal interests, as opposed to the best interests of our country, and he must be held accountable for potential wrongdoing. No one is above the law, including the President of the United States." She added that the president's actions were "not only irresponsible, but potentially illegal" and for this reason needed to be fully investigated by Congress.

The article continued by pointing out the Jewish Congress members who were strongly supporting the impeachment inquiry:

Rep. Adam Schiff, Chair of the House Intelligence Committee, went after the president Wednesday, comparing his actions to a 'mafia boss.' "There was only one message that the President of Ukraine got from that call, and that was: 'This is what I need, I know what you need,'" Schiff said. "Like any mafia boss, the president didn't need to say, 'That's a nice country you have, it'd be a shame if something happened to it.'" The Jewish Florida Rep. Ted Deutch backed Pelosi. "Trump asked the Ukrainian president to manufacture dirt on his political opponent," he tweeted. "This cannot be acceptable behavior in our democracy. Seeking campaign help from a foreign government is a corrupt abuse of power and violates the president's oath of office." Senate Minority leader Chuck Schumer, also Jewish, voiced support for the move. "The events of recent days have brought sharply into focus the question of whether the President of the United States abused the powers of his office and betrayed the public trust for personal political gain," he said on Wednesday during a Senate speech. "We need all the facts. I strongly support Speaker Pelosi's decision." https://www.jpost.com/American-Politics/Jewish-Democrats-express-support-for-impeachment-inquiry-against-Trump-602760

Will the impeachment be seen by Trump's base as being orchestrated by the Jews? It's true that Nancy Pelosi is not Jewish and that there are only 32 Jewish Congress members out of 435 (about 7.4%). But the prominence of Schiff as the chair of the House Intelligence Committee and the leader of the effort, along with Nadler, head of the House Judiciary Committee and a longtime Trump "foe," give a strong Jewish "flavor" to the effort. Also, the representation of Jews in prominent positions of the liberal, anti-Trump media gave the American Jewish community a prominent profile and outsized impact in the impeachment.

There is a small percentage of Republicans and independents in the American Jewish community. But, in spite of this somewhat pro-Trump minority among American Jews, Trump supporters view the American Jewish community as powerful, liberal, and dedicated to bringing Trump down. In a time where anti-Semitism is on the rise and when, for the first time in generations, Jewish blood has been spilled on the streets of America by those who feel threatened by liberal policies, especially toward immigration, we must at least consider the potential impact that the impeachment of Trump could contribute to inflaming anti-Jewish sentiment in the U.S. In an August 2017 *Atlantic* magazine article, "Why Charlottesville Marchers Were Obsessed with Jews," Emma Green writes:

> In the world sketched by white supremacists, Jews hover malevolently in the background, pulling strings, controlling events, acting as an all-powerful force backing and enabling the other targets of their hate. That's clear in statements made by people like Duke, the former Ku Klux Klan leader who proudly marched with other white supremacists in Charlottesville. Jewish Zionists, he complained to a gathered crowd, control the media and American political system.
> https://www.theatlantic.com/politics/archive/2017/08/nazis-racism-charlottesville/536928/

It is true that Jewish Congress members only made up a small percentage of the politicians who would impeach Trump. But Jewish participation in the process is significant and prominent *enough* for concern that those who have long believed that the Jews are "pulling the strings" of society, will blame the Jews for the attempt to crucify their "savior" (sound familiar?); that the Jews seek to delegitimize the "Chosen One" who Trumpsters view as miraculously achieving the highest office of the land, and who has been chosen to protect them from a rising left tide in which they see themselves marginalized, demonized, and abused.

Is this concern just a bit of Jewish paranoia due to the Jewish people long being blamed for nefarious acts they didn't do? (poisoning of wells during the black plague, murdering Christian children for ritualistic purposes, destroying the German economy after World War 1, the 9/11 attack, etc.). I hope so. But there is a fervor about some of Trump's diehard supporters as displayed at his rallies that gives one pause. Also, the unprecedented demonizing of liberal and left policies by Trumpland is another concern if one is part of the country's high profile liberal/left demographics. A December 19, 2019 article in the Times of Israel voiced a similar concern:

> But to far-right anti-Semitic extremists, there's been something else entirely driving the president's woes: a cabal of powerful Jews determined to oust him from office. Last month, the founder of TruNews, a fundamentalist Christian platform that regularly publishes anti-Semitic and racist videos, raged against a "Jew coup" to impeach Trump. Many of the officials involved in the impeachment inquiry — such as California Congressman Adam Schiff, New York Congressman Jerry Nadler, and witness to the probe Trump's US Ambassador to the European Union Gordon Sondland, among others — are Jewish. "That's the way the Jews work, they are deceivers, they plot, they lie, they do whatever they have to do to accomplish their political agenda," said Pastor Rick Wiles. In the past few weeks, that conspiracy theory has only been

growing on the internet's anti-Semitic fringe. The Unz Review, an anti-Semitic platform, ran a story titled "Trump Woos Jews, Jews Impeach Trump," which argued that "the impeachment farce is basically a Jewish affair." The piece, written by the anti-Semitic Swedish writer Israel Shamir, criticized Trump for pandering to the Jews through his Israel policy, only to be betrayed by them. "Trump thought that his generosity would melt Jewish hearts, and they would let him govern in peace," Shamir writes. "But no, the Jews accept every gift as their due." According to experts who track anti-Semitic incidents in the United States, over the last several months this type of rhetoric has become more commonplace among far-right corners of the internet. "We've seen many anti-Semites latching onto this conspiracy narrative that Jews are playing a conspiratorial role in trying to oust the duly elected president of the United States for the Jews' own nefarious reasons," said Aryeh Tuchman, associate director of the Anti-Defamation League's Center for Extremism. "These are all hardcore anti-Semites who thankfully exist on the fringes of society, but the fear is that these anti-Jewish conspiracy theories will gain more traction with the broader public," Tuchman told The Times of Israel. "This is particularly true with Rick Wiles. He has quite a large audience for his shows."

https://www.timesofisrael.com/jew-coup-the-anti-semitic-conspiracy-theories-surrounding-trumps-impeachment/

As the 2020 election looms we will see whether this newest of Jewish conspiracy theories remains an insignificant fringe positions or if it works its way towards the mainstream, exacerbated and energized by a hard fought election and a broken economy that will most likely take years to recover from the devastating effects of the COVID-19 pandemic.

Chapter 20

The Jewish Face of Trump's Impeachment Inquiry and Trial

Donald Trump has been impeached by the U.S. House of Representative—only the third president to have been so disgraced along with Andrew Johnson and Bill Clinton. After a strategically unsuccessful delay by the Speaker of the House, Nancy Pelosi signed the articles of impeachment and they were transferred to the Senate on January 15, 2020. President Trump was impeached by the U.S. House of Representatives for "Abuse of Power" and "Obstruction of Justice." The articles were submitted and signed by Congressman Jerry Nadler, Head of Justice Committee.

Regarding "Abuse of Power" the articles state:

> Using the powers of his high office, President Trump solicited the Interference of a foreign government, Ukraine, in the 2020 United States Presidential election. He did so through a

> scheme or course of conduct that included soliciting the Government of Ukraine to publicly announce investigations that would benefit his reelection, harm the election prospects of a political opponent, and influence the 2020 United States Presidential election to his advantage.

Regarding "Obstruction of Justice" the articles state:

> Donald J. Trump has directed the unprecedented, categorical, and indiscriminate defiance of subpoenas issued by the House of Representatives pursuant to its "sole Power of Impeachment'.' President Trump has abused the powers of the Presidency in a manner offensive to, and subversive of, the Constitution

The full text of the Articles of Impeachment is about 1,200 words and can be found at this link: https://www.documentcloud.org/documents/6572303-Articles-of-Impeachment.html

It is also worthy of note that the three legal experts called to testify at the impeachment trial were all Jewish:

- Harvard University Professor Noah Feldman
- Stanford University Professor Pamela Karlan
- University of North Carolina Professor Michael Gerhardt

All three were all asked, based on the House Intelligence Committee evidence, "Did President Trump commit the impeachable high crime and misdemeanor of abuse of power?" All said that he did.

The Senate Trial

The impeachment trial took place in the Republican-controlled Senate where Majority Leader Mitch McConnell had control of the process in a Senate "court" presided over by Chief Justice John Roberts. But the Democratic House of Representatives still played an active role. House Speaker Pelosi chose seven House Democrats to make the case for impeachment before the Senate. These "Impeachment Managers" were:

- House Intelligence Committee Chairman Adam Schiff
- House Judiciary Committee Chairman Jerry Nadler
- Congresswoman Zoe Lofgren
- Congressman Hakeem Jeffries
- Congresswoman Val Demings
- Congressman Jason Crow
- Congresswoman Sylvia Garcia

Adam Schiff was the lead impeachment manager and highly visible in the Senate trial with multiple, hours-long presentations debating various Democratic amendments requesting witnesses and documents, which were voted down by the Senators strictly along party lines. Jerry Nadler was also prominently featured in presentations along with the other impeachment managers. So, although the shift to the Senate put the Republicans in control of the process, the House of Representatives' Jewish leadership was still quite front and center with Adam Schiff and Jerry Nadler leading the charge.

The Trump Defense team leadership was made up of:

1-Pat Cipollone. He was the White House counsel that headed Trump's defense team. A staunch Catholic, he was a founding member of the National Catholic Prayer Breakfast and had the novel distinction of having converted conservative commentator Laura Ingraham to Catholicism.

2-Jay Sekolow. He was the second-in-command of the president's defense, and was previously the coordinator of

Trump's personal legal team in his defense during former Special Counsel Robert Mueller's investigations. Sekolow was born Jewish in Brooklyn but converted to Messianic Judaism after encountering Jews for Jesus.

3-Ken Starr, who was previously the head of the Whitewater investigation of President Clinton and had provided legal counsel on many major cases. Starr is the son of a Texas minister, and he attended the Churches of Christ, which is affiliated with Harding University in Searcy, Arkansas.

4-Alan Dershowitz was also a member of the Trump defense team and stated that he would "present oral arguments at the Senate trial to address the constitutional arguments against impeachment and removal." Dershowitz, an emeritus professor of law at Harvard, is a constitutional and criminal law scholar and is known for his staunch defense of civil liberties and individual rights. He is also an author, popular pundit, and staunch defender of Israel.

Personally, I am pleased that there was a Jewish presence on Trump's defense team as it dilutes the impression that the Jewish community is united in its desire to remove Trump from office. True, the vast majority of Jewish Americans are Democrats and liberals and do favor Trump's removal, but the optics are better in that there were Jews who were defending him as well and making arguments for his acquittal and continuing as president. As has been discussed throughout this book, optics are very important to the level of anti-Semitism in America—perhaps more than the actual facts. So, thank you, Alan and Jay for helping to reduce the impression that this was a "Jewish impeachment." And although Jay Sekolow is a Messianic and many would not consider him Jewish, I still think that for optics sake, he definitely made the grade.

<u>Witnesses and Documents</u>

The major issue that was at play in the Senate impeachment trial was whether they would subpoena witnesses and relevant documents that were not made available in the House impeachment. Trump refused to allow a number of witnesses subpoenaed by the Democrats in the House to testify and refused to produce subpoenaed documents.

The 17 witnesses who did not "show up" and defied subpoena were:

- Mike Pence, Vice President
- Mick Mulvaney, Acting White House Chief of Staff
- Robert Blair, Top Aid to Acting White House Chief of Staff
- John Bolton, former National Security Advisor
- Charles Kupperman, former Deputy National Security Advisor
- John Eisenberg, Top National Security Council Attorney
- Michael Ellis, Deputy National Security Council Legal Adviser
- Wells Griffith, Trump Adviser on Energy and Climate
- Mark T. Esper, Defense Secretary
- Russel T. Vought, Acting Budget Director
- Michael Duffey, White House Budget Official
- Pick Perry, Energy Secretary
- Brian McCormack, Former Chief of Staff to the Energy Secretary
- Mike Pompeo, Secretary of State
- John J. Sullivan, Deputy Secretary of State
- T. Ulrich Brechbuhl, Former Adviser to Mike Pompeo
- Rudolph Giuliani, President Trump's Personal Attorney

There were 16 witnesses that did appear in the impeachment trial, the most impactful being:

- Fiona Hill, former Trump Adviser on Russia
- Timothy Morrison, former Trump Adviser on Russia
- Lieutenant Colonel Alexander S. Vindman, National Security Council official
- Joseph Maguire, Acting Director of National Intelligence
- David Hale, Undersecretary of State for Political Affairs
- Gordon D. Sondland, Ambassador to the E.U.
- Willaim B. Taylor Jr., Top American Diplomat in Ukraine
- Kurt D. Volker, former Special Envoy to Ukraine
- Marie L. Yovanovitch, former Ambassador to Ukraine

The documents that House Democrats assessed as relevant to the impeachment inquiry were not produced at the instruction of the White House. Three of the House committees requested Vice President Pence provide them with documents, though no subpoena had been issued. Refusals from top administration officials followed the White House counsel's office, sending a letter to top Democrats stating that the administration would refuse to cooperate with the impeachment inquiry. Matthew Morgan, counsel to the vice president, wrote in a letter to the three committee chairmen that Pence would not comply with their request, citing the lack of a vote establishing formal procedures for the impeachment inquiry and questioning the fairness of the process. A letter from Giuliani's lawyer to the House Intelligence Committee dismissed the subpoena,

saying it is "overbroad, unduly burdensome, and seeks documents beyond the scope of legitimate inquiry."

The Pentagon said in a letter to the three committee leaders that it had taken steps to identify and preserve potentially relevant documents, but that the subpoena "raises a number of legal and practical concerns" and the department would not comply "at this time." A senior administration official said that OMB and acting Director Russ Vought "are not participating in the sham impeachment process."

There was a glimmer of hope by Democrats that the Senate would allow witnesses and request documents, but in the end on January 31, 2020, the vote was 51 against and 49 for calling witnesses. Only two Republican senators voted to call witnesses—Mitt Romney of Utah and Susan Collins of Maine. A majority vote was required to move the calling of witnesses forward. This vote effectively ended the trial with an acquittal vote set up for the following week. The acquittal vote took place on February 5 with the following outcome:

Impeachment Impact on the American Jewish Community
Has the impeachment put a chink in Donald Trump's armor and convinced some on the fence to fall to the left? Will it fire up his base and convince others that there is a conspiracy of the left that must be defeated? The election is almost upon us and there will be endless analysis of how the impeachment impacted the outcome, whatever it turns out to be.

But what about the impact of the impeachment on the Jewish community? More particularly, how has the impeachment affected the perception of the American Jews by Americans who are not Jewish? For those on the left, the Jewish presence in the process will be viewed in a positive light. The older, less radical, liberal Democrats to whom Schumer, Schiff and Nadler belong, may have gained a bit of cred among the Sanders camp and other far left members of the party. I think in part, this is why Pelosi decided to go ahead with the impeachment despite her obvious reticence. Personally, I think we have witnessed the marginalizing of the moderate Democrats from the party leadership as Bernie and his minions grow in size and strength and the more extreme left positions are favored by younger Democratic voters.

But what about the rest of America? How was this political drama perceived by the Trumpers and Republicans, as well as those with moderate and conservative views? For those with conspiratorial perspectives I think it strengthened their conviction that the Jews are at the center of these imagined conspiracies—"pulling the strings," so to speak, to impose a universalist, liberal culture on America through government, media, and corporate structure. Trump is viewed by many of these conspiracy believers as the "chosen one" who has the strength and bluster to defeat what they see as a Jewish takeover of their country and the world. The impeachment will be seen by them as just part of a larger process to crucify their savior.

More importantly, how will the impeachment impact the view of the Jewish community among what I will call the moderate to conservative group, who do not tend to believe in conspiracy theories or take extreme positions? How will impeachment move the needle for them? Well, the impeachment certainly didn't hurt Trump's approval ratings among Republicans. If this is an indication, it would seem that the impeachment may be viewed by this larger group of Americans as an unjustified attack on Trump—basically a political hit job. Although this larger, more reasonable group of Republicans and conservatives may not see the impeachment as part of an international Jewish plot, it will not be lost on them that Jewish congressional representatives and Jewish legal experts were at the forefront of what they view as an elaborate smear campaign. For some, it may stimulate at least a political anti-Semitism, if not a more general disdain for the Jewish people.

But the most important impact of the impeachment is whether it will help Trump be re-elected or help whoever the Democratic nominee will be to achieve victory in November. Whatever the outcomes, I don't think we are at the end of this chapter in American politics, as the impeachment will continue to play a major role in the presidential contest with both Trump and Biden using it as a cudgel for these attacks on one another. Trump will portray it as the most apparent symbol of the liberal conspiracy to negate his being duly elected president, and the Democrats and liberals as the clearest evidence of his criminality and unfitness for our country's highest position.

Chapter 21

Trump, Governmental Lawlessness, and the Jewish (Not So) Civil War

King Solomon wrote:

> To everything there is a season.... A time to love. A time to hate. A time for war. A time for peace.

But just what is "a time for peace"? Is it a time when there are no conflicts between different groups in a society? I don't think so. Peace can reign within conflict, but only when there is enough common ground to respect and work with your opponent toward a shared objective. On the other hand, a time of war is when there is a sense that your opponent is so unreasonable or downright evil that collaborative efforts are seen as unable to accomplish anything positive. In a time of war, each side simply wants to emerge victorious and destroy the opponent.

During a time of war, no effort is exerted toward building bridges, explaining the reasonableness of one's positions to the other side, or attempting to see an issue from the opponent's point of view. During a physical war, the desire is not peace, but the physical subjugation of the enemy. During a political war, the objective is similar. Perhaps no blood is spilled, but the goal is still to render the other side as diminished as possible and to remove its impact from governance. In a time of political war, the strategy is not to convince the uncommitted to join your side. Instead, it is to fire up your base by demonizing the enemy as much as possible.

Here we are closing in on the 2020 presidential elections and we find ourselves post-impeachment with a widened chasm dividing the country by party and pro- versus anti-Trumpers. (*All congressional Republicans voted against the impeachment and all but two congressional Democrats voted in favor of it* In the Senate vote Mitt Romney was the only Republican who voted to convict the president. Saying the president committed "an appalling abuse of the public trust," Utah Republican Senator Mitt Romney voted to convict President Donald Trump on the first article of impeachment, becoming the first senator ever to vote against his own party's president in an impeachment trial. The Senate voted 52-48 to acquit on the first article, and 53-47 on the second. Romney voted to acquit on the second charge, obstruction of Congress.

About 150 years ago Abraham Lincoln famously stated:

> A house divided against itself, cannot stand. I believe this government cannot endure, permanently, half slave and half free. I do not expect the Union to be dissolved—I do not expect the house to fall—but I do expect it will cease to be divided. It will become all one thing or all the other.

Lincoln was describing the deep divide between the North and South over slavery, which did result in America's most bloody conflict and its only civil war. Although we are not currently divided on an issue as fundamental or clearly defined as slavery, Lincoln's statement expresses the idea that there are limits to the level of conflict between opposing groups that a country can endure and continue to function as a single nation. There are indications that the United States of America and its people may no longer be functioning as a coherent polity. There is a growing governmental lawlessness on the federal, state, and local level.

The Increase in Governmental Lawlessness

The depth of animosity and disdain currently in play between the right and the left, and between the Democratic and the Republican parties, has resulted in a growing disregard for the rule of law at various levels of government. Usually we think of lawlessness as being something that governments prevent and control. But recently we are experiencing a strange phenomenon: the population is basically law-abiding, but the government, in many cases, is not! This is occurring on both the left and right.

President Trump and Lawlessness

The president is viewed by many (about half of the U.S. population) as someone who breaks the law on a regular basis. Many on the left, and even a few on the right, have accused him of violating one or more of the following laws:

Bribery. The use of government office powers in exchange for personal gain is attributed to Trump by many in his tying of Ukrainian military aid to a public investigation of Joe Biden and his son's involvement in Burista (a Ukrainian energy company). This was the basis of the impeachment of the president.

Campaign Finance Law Violation. Michael Cohen's paying off of Stormy Daniels with Trump's campaign funds and Trump not reporting it would violate the law. Trump was not convicted of this crime and denied any wrongdoing. Michael Cohen, Trump's longtime personal attorney and "fixer," did plead guilty to two violations of the Federal Election Campaign Law, the law that governs the financing of federal election campaigns, and served time in jail.

Collusion/Conspiracy. Many believe that Trump is guilty of conspiracy, assuming that he approved the meeting between his son, Donald Trump Jr.; son-in-law, Jared Kushner; campaign chairman, Paul Manafort; and a Russian lawyer who claimed to have "dirt" on Hillary Clinton. Regarding this, Jens David Ohlin, a law professor and vice dean at Cornell Law School, wrote in *The Atlantic*:

> This reeks of a criminal conspiracy. It doesn't even matter if nothing came of the meeting [although that's far from clear]. If Trump knew about the meeting and was okay with it, Trump and those around him could be guilty of an inchoate conspiracy."…
> If Trump approved a meeting with foreign nationals in the hopes of obtaining something of value—i.e., opposition research at the height of the presidential election—the intent alone could provide prosecutors with an important piece in understanding the campaign's willingness to conspire with Russia, legal experts told me.
> https://www.theatlantic.com/politics/archive/2018/07/trump-michael-cohen-trump-tower-meeting/566303/

Violation of the Emoluments Clause. The Foreign Emoluments Clause was placed in the Constitution to keep federal officials from being improperly influenced by or beholden to foreign governments. The clause provides that no federal officers can "without the Consent of the Congress, accept of any present, Emolument, Office, or Title, of any kind whatever, from any King, Prince, or foreign State." There are numerous cases of President Trump suggesting or requesting assistance from Russia, China, and Ukraine in ways that appear, to many, to personally benefit him. Also, the use of Trump-owned properties for many federal government meetings and activities and its frequent use by foreign officials has raised eyebrows. Whether this actually violates the Emoluments Clause is questionable (some hold the law doesn't apply to the president), but the unprecedented level of personal profit entwined with the presidency of Donald Trump is unseemly and its legality is certainly debatable. In *The Hill* article "Trump may be haunted by 'phony' Emoluments Clause," it states:

> As for Russia, it has been established by the Mueller report that Russia interfered in the 2016 U.S. presidential election. Candidate Trump welcomed their assistance in his "Russia, if you are listening…" appeal in July 2016 to hack Democratic presidential nominee Hillary Clinton's emails. The acceptance of a present can be established by words and deeds that tell the giver that the present is welcome. There is no need to prove collusion, conspiracy, solicitation, or quid pro quo. There is a strong body of evidence that President Trump has conveyed to Russian President Vladimir Putin that he welcomes Russia's assistance and, if reelected in 2020, will be grateful. First is President Trump's 2017 Oval Office meeting with Russian Foreign Minister Sergei Lavrov and Russian Ambassador Sergey Kislyak the day after he fired former FBI director James Comey. As reported in The Washington Post, the president told the Russians that the firing relieved "great pressure" on him related to Russia, and he made clear that he was not concerned about Russian interference in the 2016 U.S. presidential election because the United States did the same in other countries. Second is the president's 2018 public statement in Putin's presence that he believed Putin's claim that he had not interfered, despite the view of the U.S. intelligence community to the contrary. Saying the interference did not happen, when the evidence shows the opposite, is a way of saying, "Keep it up, and you will hear no criticism from me."
> https://thehill.com/opinion/white-house/469060-trump-may-be-haunted-by-phony-emoluments-clause

Obstruction of Justice. CBS News journalist Will Rahn wrote on July 23, 2019, in his article "10 times Trump may have obstructed justice, according to Mueller":

> Although the special counsel's report on Russian interference does not come to a conclusion as to whether President Trump obstructed justice, Robert Mueller's team did

examine 10 "discrete acts" in which he may have done so. The report says these 10 instances can be divided into "two phases, reflecting a possible shift in the president's motives." The first phase took place before Mr. Trump fired his first FBI director, James Comey, after he had been reassured he was not personally under investigation. After Comey's dismissal and Mueller's appointment as special counsel, the report indicates, the president knew he was now under investigation for possibly obstructing justice, and switched gears. At that point, the president engaged in a second phase of conduct, involving public attacks on the investigation, non-public efforts to control it, and efforts both in public and private to encourage witnesses not to cooperate with the investigation," the report list these 10 possible instances of obstruction of justice:

1. Conduct involving FBI Director Comey and Michael Flynn
2. The President's reaction to the continuing Russia investigation
3. The President's termination of Comey
4. The appointment of Special Counsel and efforts to remove him
5. Efforts to curtail the Special Counsel's investigation
6. Efforts to prevent public disclosure of evidence
7. Further efforts to have the Attorney General take control of the investigation
8. Efforts to have McGahn deny that the President had ordered him to have the Special Counsel removed
9. Conduct toward Flynn, Manafort, [Redacted]
10. Conduct involving Michael Cohen

A description of each of these 10 issues is provided in the article, which can be accessed through the following link:

https://www.cbsnews.com/news/obstruction-of-justice-10-times-trump-may-have-obstructed-justice-mueller-report/

But despite this lengthy list of possibly illegal and certainly questionable activities, where President Trump contributes most to a growing sense of lawlessness in our country, is with his tone and choice of words. His insulting, aggressive rally speeches and endless Tweets directed against his opponents makes a mockery of the graciousness, maturity, and polite decorum that is usually associated with the office of President of the United States. And it is not only what Trump says, it is how he says it. He has no concern at all for spelling or grammar or any sense of linguistic propriety, even at a surface level. Some previously unimaginable examples of the leader of the free world communicating with his governmental officials and the public include:

1-Why are we having all these people from sh—hole countries come here?

2 We have the worst laws.

3-Why would Kim Jong-un insult me by calling me "old," when I would NEVER call him "short and fat."

4-Lightweight Senator Kirsten Gillibrand, a total flunky for Chuck Schumer and someone who would come to my office "begging" for campaign contributions not so long ago (and would do anything for them), is now in the ring fighting against Trump. Very disloyal to Bill & Crooked-USED!

5- Any negative polls are fake news, just like the CNN, ABC, NBC polls in the election.

6-I heard poorly rated @MorningJoe speaks badly of me (don't watch anymore). Then how come low I.Q. Crazy Mika, along with Psycho Joe, came (to a party at Trump' Mar-a-Lago resort).

7-Actually, throughout my life, my two greatest assets have been mental stability and being, like, really smart. Crooked Hillary Clinton also played these cards very hard and, as everyone knows, went down in flames. I went from VERY successful businessman, to top T.V. Star to President of the United States (on my first try). I think that would qualify as not smart, but genius....and a very stable genius at that!

8-Russia, if you're listening, I hope you're able to find the 30,000 emails that are missing. I think you will probably be rewarded mightily by our press.

9-North Korean Leader Kim Jong Un just stated that the 'Nuclear Button is on his desk at all times.' Will someone from his depleted and food starved regime please inform him

that I too have a Nuclear Button, but it is a much bigger &
more powerful one than his, and my Button works!

10-Wouldn't you love to see one of these NFL owners, when
somebody disrespects our flag, to say, 'Get that son of a bitch
off the field right now. Out! He's fired, he's fired!'"

11-[John McCain's] not a war hero. He's a war hero because
he was captured. I like people who weren't captured.

12- Yeah, she's really something, and what a beauty, that one.
If I weren't happily married and, ya know, her father…
(about dating his daughter Ivanka)

If these whacko statements do not strike you as being outrageous
coming from the president of the United States, it shows how
much Trump has moved the ball of civilized behavior in our
country.

Trickle-down Lawlessness in the Executive Branch

There have been many members of the Executive branch who
refused to answer congressional subpoenas to testify in the
impeachment inquiry. These included:

- John Eisenberg, Legal Adviser to the National Security
  Council
- Michael Ellis, Deputy Legal Adviser to the National
  Security Council
- Robert Blair, Aide to acting White House Chief of Staff
  Mick Mulvaney
- Brian McCormack, Aide to the White House Office of
  Management and Budget
- Donald McGahn, former White House Counsel
- John Bolton, former National Security Advisor

Are these individuals in violation of the law? It is true that
Congress has the broad rights to require testimony or documents
and those who refuse may be found to be in "Contempt of

Congress," which is a federal misdemeanor punishable by a maximum $100,000 fine and a maximum one-year sentence in federal prison. But a subpoenaed individual can claim executive privilege if the testimony is regarding issues that are sensitive or confidential communications within the executive branch. In addition, the enforcement of the "Contempt of Congress" penalty is in the hands of the Executive branch of government, and if it is not inclined to pursue criminal charges against the person who ignores the subpoena, it will be difficult or perhaps impossible to prosecute these individuals. Although it is possible that a court would find these refusals to answer a subpoena justified, the way it appears and is portrayed by the Democratic-led Congress is that these government officials are simply flouting the law. The general presentation by mainstream media is that we are viewing a defiance of the power of Congress by the executive branch—in essence, an appearance of governmental lawlessness.

State and Municipal Lawlessness

The Trump administration accused "sanctuary cities" of lawlessness in refusing to cooperate with federal Immigration and Customs Enforcement (ICE) agents in apprehending illegal aliens who have been identified as subject to capture and removal. The official US Department of Homeland Security website states:

> Under federal law, ICE has the authority to lodge immigration detainers with law enforcement partners who have custody of individuals arrested on criminal charges and who ICE has probable cause to believe are removable aliens. The detainer form asks the other law enforcement agency to notify ICE in advance of release and to maintain custody of the alien for a brief period so that ICE can take custody of that person in a safe and secure setting upon release from that agency's custody. Across the United States, several jurisdictions refuse to honor detainers and instead choose to willingly release criminal offenders back into their local communities where they are free to offend.

The term "Sanctuary City" refers to a city or state that enacts policies that are favorable to illegal immigrants and prevent inquiries into a person's immigration status, unless they are a suspect of crime or have been deported in the past. For example, on October 5, 2017, Governor Jerry Brown signed a bill, the California Sanctuary Law SB54, that makes California a "sanctuary state." It prohibits local and state agencies from cooperating with ICE regarding illegal criminals who have committed misdemeanors. According to the National Immigration Law Center in 2016, about a dozen California cities have some formal sanctuary policy, and none of the 58 California counties complies with detainer requests by U.S. Immigration and Customs Enforcement.

In the state of New York, the cities of Albany, Ithaca, and New York City as well as Franklin, Nassau, Onondaga, and St. Lawrence counties are sanctuary areas. In late 2014, New York Mayor Bill de Blasio signed two bills into law that significantly reduced the degree to which city officials would cooperate with federal immigration enforcement. The introductions 486-A and 487-A ended New York City's law enforcement cooperation with Immigration and Customs Enforcement detainer requests, except in situations where an individual has been convicted of a violent crime. The bills also ended the presence of federal immigration officials at Rikers Island and all other city-run facilities. The city is home to more than 500,000 illegal aliens, according to recent estimates.

The legality of the states' non-cooperative actions is complex. Put simply, the states, with some exceptions, are not required to carry out federal law if they do not choose to do so. However, they cannot interfere with federal authorities carrying out those federal laws in the state. Where exactly different state and city policies fall within this spectrum is an issue for debate and court action. The Trump administration has filed numerous lawsuits against states and cities regarding these "Sanctuary City" policies. For example, the U.S. Department of Justice Office of Public Affairs sent out a "Demand for Documents" to 23 sanctuary jurisdictions. The U.S. Department of Justice website published the following regarding this "Demand for Documents":

> FOR IMMEDIATE RELEASE, Wednesday, January 24, 2018
> Justice Department Demands Documents and Threatens to Subpoena 23 Jurisdictions As Part of 8 U.S.C. 1373 Compliance Review.
>
> The Department of Justice today sent the attached letters to 23 jurisdictions, demanding the production of documents that could show whether each jurisdiction is unlawfully restricting information sharing by its law enforcement officers with federal immigration authorities. All 23 of these jurisdictions were previously contacted by the Justice Department, when the Department raised concerns about laws, policies, or practices that may violate 8 U.S.C. 1373, a federal statute that promotes information sharing related to immigration enforcement and with which compliance is a condition of FY2016 and FY2017 Byrne JAG awards. The letters also state that recipient jurisdictions that fail to respond, fail to respond completely, or fail to respond in a timely manner will be subject to a Department of Justice subpoena.

Lawlessness, Anti-Semitism, and its Impact on the American Jewish Community

As a rule, during the 2,000 years of its diaspora, the Jewish people have suffered greatly from lawlessness in the societies in which they have lived. Crusades, massacres, pogroms, and mass violence and vandalism against the Jewish community has been a repeated tragic motif in its history. It is true that sometimes a country's laws themselves have proved damaging or dangerous to its Jewish residents, but more often it is the prevalence of (often tolerated) lawlessness that has resulted in Jewish suffering. In the Mishnaic work "The Ethics of the Fathers" it states:

Rabbi Chanina, the deputy High Priest taught, "Pray for the government, for were it not for the fear of it, men would swallow one another alive." (Ethics of the Fathers, 3:2)

Regardless of the Jewish community's success in American society, its wealth, small size, and distinct character make it a prime target of many groups in the event that lawlessness in the government translates to a similar dysfunction on the public level. The synagogue killings in Pittsburgh and Poway, California, are examples of what can happen when a sense of lawlessness combines with a profound partisan animosity toward the other side.

Lawlessness is not simply a disorderly, anarchic phenomenon. It can also be a reaction to a situation where people view the laws as deeply unjust or destructive. We see "ideological lawlessness" in many areas including environmental groups such as Greenpeace and anti-fascist groups such as Antifa. Regardless of whether a Jewish person is on the right or on the left, whether pro- or anti-Trump, disregard for law and even for political decorum is a threat to his or her peaceful co-existence in the society. This consideration should be taken into account when Jewish groups act to support or fight against a particular issue or politician.

Donald Trump and the Jewish Community's War Against Itself
Are opposing sides in the Jewish community civilly disagreeing, or are things heating up to the point where a warlike lawlessness is entering the fray with each group simply wanting to quash the other? Are the Jews on the left and on the right presently working together in any meaningful capacity on shared Jewish community issues?

There is little doubt that the presidency of Donald Trump and the rise of intersectionalism on the left has deepened the animosity of Jewish liberals for Jewish Trumpers and vice versa. Intersectionalism has linked multiple liberal causes into a single position, so that if one is not anti-Zionist (now a core left position) one cannot really be anti-discrimination or anti-oppression. This issue has been particularly relevant in the younger Jewish demographics and on the college/university campuses. The situation is described by columnist Jonathan S. Tobin, editor-in-chief of *JNS*, in his February 2019 article "Liberal Zionists must take up the fight against BDS, not ally with it," in which he writes:

There was a time when Israel and the organized Jewish world didn't hesitate about supporting left-wing Jewish student groups. Back in the late 1960s and early 1970s, groups like the North American Jewish Students Network were often harshly critical of the government led by Israeli Prime Minister Golda Meir in the years after the Six-Day War. But Meir and her colleagues still considered such groups to be allies in the struggle to defend Israel against an Arab world that was determined to stick to its stance of "no peace, no recognition and no negotiations" with the Jewish state... Flash-forward 50 years later and some still make the same claim. The conceit of the J Street lobby is that it is following in the footsteps of those students with its "pro-Israel, pro-peace" mantra. J Street thinks its critiques of the Netanyahu government give it the standing to speak for the tradition of liberal Zionism

that is in tune with the political leanings of the vast majority of American Jews. J Street argues that if the only voices speaking up for Israel are those identified with the Israeli right or supporters of the Trump administration, then it will turn off young Jews. Youth culture in the United States skews hard to the left, making any cause that isn't somehow linked with progressive orthodoxy to be beyond the pale. Radical anti-Zionist groups like Students for Justice in Palestine (SJP), and their Jewish auxiliaries at IfNotNow and Jewish Voice for Peace (JVP), maintain a strong presence on many campuses these days. As a result, liberals believe that only groups with a progressive orientation like J Street U, which is deeply critical of Israeli policies while still claiming to be pro-Zionist, can effectively represent Jewish interests and, in effect, save Jewish youth for the pro-Israel camp. It makes sense. Or at least, it would if that's actually what J Street U was doing. In the past few years, there have been many reported instances in which J Street U chapters have made common cause with SJP or JVP in criticizing the efforts of pro-Israel groups like the Maccabee Task Force or Hillel in order to castigate those organizing trips to Israel

or holding events with Zionist speakers. In many other instances, J Street U chapters have jointly sponsored events with SJP or JVP groups… It's still true that for many young Jews, anything that can be branded as non-progressive—let alone pro-Trump or pro-Netanyahu—is anathema to their worldview.
https://www.jns.org/opinion/liberal-zionists-must-take-up-the-fight-against-bds-not-ally-with-it/

Another take on the depth of the expanding Jewish communal divide is explored in a November 2018 *Guardian* article by Ed Vulliamy:

> Not within living memory has America been so divided but neither has its Jewish community. As an op-ed in America's oldest Jewish magazine, the Forward—which celebrated its 120th anniversary last year—said in the aftermath of Pittsburgh and the midterm elections: "the American Jewish community is asking itself for the first time in half a century: What does it mean to be a Jew in America?" The divide in America's Jewish community is in ever-sharper focus. Trump is hailed by some in America's Jewish community for his support of Israel, moving the US embassy from Tel Aviv to Jerusalem and his tearing up of the Iran deal brokered by Barack Obama. But he is repudiated by more people within that same community for his rhetorical violence and the succour he is seen to give to the far right and white nationalists. That divide has only grown since the shooting in Pittsburgh…. The rift within Jewry cuts not only along party lines; the other great divide—not entirely in parallel—is over Israel, the current politics of Israel, and what is happening in the Middle East…. Though Jews have traditionally voted Democrat, Trump's antisemitic support cuts like a rip-tide beneath those figures now…. Trump seems to have something of an affirmative prejudice toward Jews. They believe he considers Jews a group of rich, smart, successful and generally powerful deal makers—all traits which Trump himself aspires to…while simultaneously touching on tropes described by historians of the topic as classically anti-Semitic.

Villiamy quotes Jonathan Weisman, a *New York Times* journalist and author of a recent book on the American Jewish community:

"On the right," writes Weisman, "anti-Semitism and militant Zionism can co-exist quite comfortably." Spencer (an Alt-Right leader-RB) calls his movement a "sort of white Zionism." In a New York Times podcast, Weisman even posits that recent racial policies by the Netanyahu government have made Israel a "model" for the alt-right on how to construct an "ethno-state." As a result of these and other deliberations, Weisman received a flurry of communications from fellow Jews that "called me an antisemite for suggesting that far-right antisemitism might have had anything to do with the atmosphere created by this president." One caller left a message for him: "It's your despicable Democrat party that's antisemitic, hate Jews like me…. You hate Jews, you hate Israel, Jonathan Weisman, you love the Iran deal by Obama to destroy Israel; you want a second Holocaust. Thank God for Trump."… —both the Pittsburgh massacre and the midterms—have created a reappraisal among parts of America's Jewish community. The arrival of congressional newcomers critical of Israel was welcomed on the pages of the Forward. Jane Eisner, editor, says that "what happened in Pittsburgh was an inflection point—maybe not a turning point—which brought forth a deep well of social justice action by American Jews that had been there all along. What's happened over the last two years is that although President Trump had done things that please the Jewish establishment—pulling out of the Iran deal, moving the embassy—this election showed 79-80% of Jews voting Democrat against him, more than Obama, far more than Clinton."…. This is "a decisive and divisive moment in American Jewish history, of divisions that reflect the divisions in America," she says. "We've had a lot of progressive Jews elected, two Democrat Jewish governors, and I think we're going to see a blossoming social justice action by Jewish Americans in response to what's happening." In his book, Weisman says: "the identity of American Jews is at a crossroads. The identification with Israel as the democracy in the Middle East comes under question with the current government, as does Trump's support for it."
https://www.theguardian.com/usnews/2018/nov/14/american-jewish-community-divisions-trump-pittsburgh

In the next few months, with the presidential election at stake, I fear the situation will heat up to an unprecedented pitch. Liberal

Jews, armed with an impeached president and a boatload of bad behavior, as Trump cranks up his demonizing of the left in order to fire up his base, will engage in a pitched battle to bring him down. Republican Jews and those few Jewish Independents and Democrats who view Trump as Israel's great protector and defender in the world, and as a bulwark against what they perceive as "far left insanity," will be fighting with equal intensity. When the battle ends, with either Trump in or out of the White House, the wounds and deepened divisions in the American Jewish community will remain, and may require years if not decades of healing, before it returns to its former level of tepid unity and functionality.

American Lawlessness, the Jewish Divide, and COVID-19

A word must be said about the impact that the domestic COVID-19 epidemic is having on the growing governmental lawlessness we have been discussing. First it should be noted that the political/ideological divide between the left and the right has efficiently absorbed the COVID-19 situation into its gaping maw. Those on the left, many from large urban areas with strong Democratic majorities, have been favoring a cautious reopening of community and economic activities in order to prevent a higher than necessary infection and mortality rate and to assure that all is done according to the best data provided by the scientific community consensus.

Dr. Anthony Fauci is an American physician, immunologist, and infectious disease specialist who has served as the director of the National Institute of Allergy and Infectious Diseases (NIAID). Since January 2020 he has been part of Trump's Coronavirus Task Force. Dr. Fauci has emerged as the champion and "last word" for the Democrats and those favoring the cautious approach to societal reopening, and who want to take their cues from the scientific community directives in charting a course out of the COVID-19 crisis. Trump and many in the Republican Party assess this cautious approach as being too timid, and while it overestimates the health risks of COVID-19, underestimates the economic impact and negative societal effects of a prolonged shutdown. At a May 21, 2020 visit to a Ford manufacturing plant in Ypsilanti, Michigan, President Trump said:

> A permanent lockdown is not a strategy for a healthy state or a healthy country. Our country wasn't meant to be shut down. We did the right thing but now it's time to open it up. A never-ending lockdown would invite a public health calamity. To protect the health of our people we must have a functioning economy.

Dr. Fauci took a different tact when he appeared before the Senate a week earlier:

> Fauci told a Senate panel last week it was "possible" that a second wave could be as bad or worse than the current situation but expressed confidence that the government's work expanding testing and contact tracing as well as producing critical medical equipment would well prepare the country to contend with future cases. "I hope that if we do have the threat of a second wave we will be able to deal with it very effectively to prevent it from becoming an outbreak not only worse than now but much, much less," Fauci said last Tuesday in virtual testimony. The top infectious disease expert also warned that reopening states too quickly would cost lives.
> https://www.msn.com/en-us/news/politics/trump-says-us-won-t-close-over-second-covid-19-wave/ar-BB14qUB5

The pressure to open up the economy, to some degree, is overwhelming, as unemployment skyrocketed to a level not seen since the Great Depression and business revenues plunged to unprecedented lows. But even as all states are beginning to resume activities that were banned during quarantine, the country is in completely uncharted territory. Will people be able to begin to return to previous activities with new rules of distancing and non-contact? This is an ongoing social experiment that has never been carried out before. Can these new laws and directives even be enforced when they are ignored or violated by a large percentage of the population? No one knows. But one thing is assured. The COVID-19 epidemic and the governmental response, whatever form it takes in the next few months has become a major flashpoint for political conflict and social skirmishes between those on the right and those on the left, be they Jewish or not.

Post George-Floyd Killing Protests

On May 25, 2020 George Perry Floyd Jr., a black American man killed during an arrest after allegedly passing a counterfeit $20 bill in Minneapolis. A video of the incident showed white police officer, Derek Chauvin, kneeling on Floyd's neck for almost eight minutes. After his death, peaceful and violent protests against police violence toward black people quickly spread across the United States and internationally. Some have been accompanied by vandalism and looting. As of this writing (7/29/20) protests have continued and spread. Federal reserves have been brought into some cities (Portland, Seattle) to protect federal buildings, leading to street battles with protesters and political battles with state and city leaders who did not request the federal assistance.

How much of this violence is a result of the COVID-19 pandemic and the high unemployment, stress and disruption of normal life is impossible to know, although it is reasonable to conclude that they are not unrelated. Regarding its impact on the Jewish community, short and long-term is also unknown. Will things return to a degree of normality and calm after the COVID-19 disaster is behind us? Has a new social reality been established regarding an assessment of racism against black people been established which will shape American views going forward? We will have to wait and see.

One speculation I will make is that George Floyd represents part of a "changing of the guard" in American moral leadership with Jewish Americans, regardless of their liberal bona fides and history of being the world most persecuted people, have further lost their credentials of as any kind of guiding light of American justice. As the Holocaust memory fades to black, the Jewish Americans are merging in the American psyche and are now viewed by the left as part of other rich, white Americans with their knee on the neck of the poor, disenfranchised and abused.

__Conclusion__

Much has changed in America since Donald Trump was elected its 45th president. The stock market rose to new heights, and unemployment dropped to new lows. By almost all measures, the economy was doing quite well. Then the coronavirus came and the boom has gone bust, at least for a while. In the middle of the coronavirus disaster, the killing of George Floyd by a Minneapolis policeman resulted in a nationwide protest against police brutality and what is widely viewed as the unequal treatment of black men by law enforcement. There have been two fatal attacks on American synagogues (Pittsburgh's Tree of Life Synagogue and the Chabad of Poway), multiple school shootings, and little progress on healthcare costs, income disparities, and immigration issues. It is also hard to remember a time when the Republican and Democratic parties were more deeply divided, and this lack of common ground has hampered progress on many pressing issues for the country.

ISIS, who was viewed as a dire international threat with a growing caliphate, has been decimated and Islamic extremist attacks in the United States and abroad are few. White supremacist violence has, unexpectedly, equaled or perhaps eclipsed Islamic extremist terror as the greatest threat to domestic tranquility. In a February 5, 2020 CBS News article, "Racially-motivated violent extremists elevated to "national threat priority," FBE director says. The director of the FBI, Christopher Wray, provided an assessment of this new domestic terrorist reality:

> The FBI has elevated its assessment of the threat posed by racially-motivated violent extremists in the U.S. to a "national threat priority" for fiscal year 2020, FBI director Christopher Wray said Wednesday. He said the FBI is placing the risk of violence from such groups "on the same footing" as threats posed to the country by foreign terrorist organizations such as ISIS and its sympathizers. "Not only is the terror threat diverse — it's unrelenting," Wray said at an oversight hearing before the House Judiciary Committee. https://www.cbsnews.com/news/racially-motivated-violent-extremism-isis-national-threat-priority-fbi-director-christopher-wray/

From a Zionist perspective there have been many noteworthy events. The U.S. Embassy was moved to Jerusalem, the Golan Heights was recognized by the U.S. as part of Israel, and the U.S. reversed its previous position of declaring that the settlements in the West Bank area are not in violation of international law.

But a more impactful transformation has taken place in America during the past three years under the Trump administration that is subtle and yet, perhaps, more profound. There is a dark subtext lurking beneath the Trump era, even in its best of times. America is a country torn in two: deeply divided and filled with people who loath one another.

There are about 55 million registered Democrats and 72 million registered Republicans. The degree of animus and disdain between these 127 million Americans is more intense than at any time since the Civil War. Even a cursory review of the polling shows them to be on polar opposite sides regarding almost every issue. What is the catalyst of this divergence in views?

Of course, it's Donald Trump.

About 90% of the Republicans love him (he was recently rated higher than Abraham Lincoln in a poll of Republicans), while 90% of the Democrats hate Trump. They hate everything about him. This is truly a unique phenomenon, and the coronavirus crisis hasn't changed this dynamic. That the same man could be viewed with such disparate assessments by intelligent people, with millions on one side judging him to be an exceptional leader and millions on the other judging him to be among the worst of humanity, is astounding. It is as if Trump has awakened deep differences in America that have laid dormant or had been long repressed.

The American Jewish community has also experienced an energizing of its differences and points of friction. The liberal Jewish focus on social justice issues and the intersectionality drive to amalgamate all of the left issues as one has made it almost impossible for the left to support Israel and Zionism and stay true to its ideals. This has put the Jewish left and liberal camps at odds with the orthodox and Israeli-American communities in the U.S. in a manner that is also unprecedented.

The 2020 Presidential Campaign

The 2020 presidential campaign will be brutal. The combination of Trump's unbounded, disparaging rhetoric, the extreme positions of those on the right and the left, and the infinite tentacles of the ubiquitous media monster will create an almost continual onslaught of fear and hate-mongering for the hapless political consumer. If you're a Democrat who thinks you hate Republicans now, just wait! If you're a Republican who sees Democrats as the harbingers of the Apocalypse, you ain't seen nothin' yet! Billions will be spent by both sides to try and make you feel the world will come to an end if you elect the opposition's candidate.

The coronavirus crisis will just add fuel to the fire with Trump supporters lauding the government's reaction and demonizing those who portray Trump as culpable for the virus's devastating impact on America. The "Fake News" charge will be extended to include "Fake Virus News," and the economic contraction will be blamed by Trumpers on what they will portray as false, conspiratorial statements and actions by the liberal/left cabal, all with the objective of depressing the economy in order to bring down Trump.

The American Jewish community will be dragged into this political war and will often be at the forefront of its battles. With leading Jewish liberals on the left fighting prominent Jewish Zionist Republicans on the right, it will be Jew versus Jew, in many cases. It will probably be ugly and bring out the worst in everyone. There is an old Jewish expression that "the evil inclination loves a fight." So, from that point of view, it may be a very entertaining year. But like many indulgences that feel invigorating at the time, the aftermath can be painful, destructive, and enduring.

What will the state of the American Jewish community be at the conclusion of 2020 with the election (or re-election) of the president? It's hard to predict. But I am sure of this. Regardless of whether Trump is re-elected or Biden becomes our 46th president, the Jewish community will be more divided and less effectual than it has been for a long time. The historic Jewish denominational divide between orthodox, conservative, reform, and unaffiliated will be intensified by this energized political divide. The American Jewish community is one that is divided against itself, and the divide will continue to widen for the foreseeable future.

About the Author

Richard Borah is a grant writer, a non-profit consultant and the author of six previous books which are all currently available on Amazon.com. He is the founder of the Observant Artist Community Circle, a non-profit organization focused on strengthening the nexus between artists and scholars. The Observant Artist Community Circle is dedicated to supporting community-oriented art projects. He lives in New York with his wife Andrea and their two daughters.

Previous publications include:

1-*Yad on the Yad:14 Analyses of Maimonides' Laws of Repentance* (2013)

2-*Understanding the Lonely Man of Faith: A Guide to Rabbi Joseph B. Soloveitchik's Essay* (2014)

3-*The Rambam and the Rav on the 54 Portions of the Torah (2015)*

4-*Creativity and the Jewish Soul - An Analysis of the 12 Torah Portions of Genesis (2016)*

5- *Creativity and the Jewish Soul- An Analysis of the 11 Torah Portions of Exodus (2017)*

6-*Understanding Halakhic Man: A Guide to Rabbi Joseph B. Soloveitchik's Essay (2018)*

www.ingramcontent.com/pod-product-compliance
Lightning Source LLC
Chambersburg PA
CBHW060823050426

42453CB00008B/570